PRAISE FOR
THE SECRET SOCIETY OF SUCCESS

"*The Secret Society of Success* is an important book that everyone should read. It is not only insightful; it's inspirational. This book captures what it really means to be successful. I am for one ready to up my game! Thank you, Tim, for giving me this gift!"

—DAVID NOVAK, COFOUNDER AND FORMER CHAIRMAN AND
CEO OF YUM! BRANDS (KFC, TACO BELL, PIZZA HUT)

"The book you're about to read is an absolute game changer, life changer, and outlook changer. It's all of those things, told in a refreshing and engaging way. It's real talk about real life, and how we can best live it out with a purpose we may have neglected or overlooked. Or maybe it's that we just got too comfortable doing things the same old way. Tim Schurrer is about to shake things up. You will never view success the same way again. And that's a very good thing."

—ERNIE JOHNSON JR., EMMY AWARD WINNER AND
HOST OF TNT'S *INSIDE THE NBA*

"Tim Schurrer is possibly the most likable person I have ever met. His natural smile and easygoing demeanor are incredibly appealing. And to say what is underneath goes against that would be untruthful. His personality and intelligence are his superpowers. In this book, Tim shares secrets for success from familiar and unfamiliar people that will translate to everyone wanting to build a life and/or business on a foundation that can't be shaken."

—SCOTT HAMILTON, OLYMPIC GOLD MEDALIST AND
NEW YORK TIMES BESTSELLING AUTHOR

"*The Secret Society of Success* is filled with truths about what it looks like to be in business to serve your employees and your community. It gives practical advice through stories of great leaders who have succeeded while never losing sight of what truly matters in life. This book will show you that it's possible to lead *and* serve with excellence."

—ANNE BEILER, FOUNDER OF AUNTIE ANNE'S

"Tim Schurrer has written a masterpiece on what defines success. It's not often that a business book is universally applicable to every person in an organization. But *The Secret Society of Success* is one of those books. Whether you're the CEO, a mid-level manager, or in an entry-level position, you can apply these simple tips to achieve even more success."

—DAVID M. R. COVEY, FORMER COO OF FRANKLINCOVEY
AND COAUTHOR OF *TRAP TALES*

"As an entrepreneur, I've chased ideas and rallied teams together to make big things happen. The way I've defined success has never been simply about revenue growth but also about using business as a pathway to impact the lives of others. This is the approach you'll learn in *The Secret Society of Success*, and it's the way to find success that is meaningful and sustainable."

—BLAKE MYCOSKIE, FOUNDER OF TOMS

"Tim has been a friend and teacher of mine for years. He makes loving and leading people look effortless even when it's not and has shown me the power of a life lived with inexplicable intention. He knows bright lights don't need spotlights. In these pages, Tim gives us a peek behind the curtain to see why and how he and other successful people get things done. *The Secret Society of Success* doesn't just point out problems in the environments we operate in, it's a handbook for addressing issues head-on with love, purpose, and perspective. Buckle up. You're going to love this book."

—BOB GOFF, *NEW YORK TIMES* BESTSELLING AUTHOR OF
LOVE DOES, EVERYBODY, ALWAYS, AND *DREAM BIG*

"*The Secret Society of Success* is an engaging, timely, and necessary book that will transform the way you think about the world and the people with whom you share it. Tim's interviews, analyses, and insights will inspire you to read and reread this book for years to come."

—ALLAN HEINBERG, SCREENWRITER OF *WONDER WOMAN,*
NETFLIX'S *THE SANDMAN,* AND ABC'S *GREY'S ANATOMY*

"With refreshing candor, Tim guides us on a fun and pragmatic journey toward true success. Tim has walked this walk unlike anyone else, and he beautifully articulates the posture and mindset that will not only change your life and work but also the world at large. This book will leave you content, fulfilled, and wanting to join the Secret Society of Success!"

—BEN MALCOLMSON, FORMER CHIEF OF STAFF FOR
PETE CARROLL, HEAD COACH OF THE SEATTLE SEAHAWKS

"Tim is an expert we can trust who has lived out every truth he is teaching. We could all benefit from a changed mindset, and this book is the vehicle that can make that happen. It will inspire, challenge, and free you to pursue your highest ideals without the chains of stale definitions and roles. It will free you to form new ideas of what success looks and feels like. Tim is offering us all a gift, be kind to yourself and accept it!"

—BECCA STEVENS, AUTHOR AND FOUNDER OF THISTLE FARMS

"The more eyes you have on you, the more challenging it can be to stay in a good headspace. Tim's take on how to define success and navigate a world obsessed with fame and status is something I think everyone—in or out of the spotlight—will benefit greatly from."

—BEN RECTOR, MUSICIAN

"Career success doesn't have to come at the expense of your relationships or your emotional well-being. *The Secret Society of Success* equips you to create your own definition of success, one that's true to your identity. Here's another tool to help you win at work and succeed at life. Well done, Tim!"

—MICHAEL HYATT, *WALL STREET JOURNAL* BESTSELLING AUTHOR
OF *WIN AT WORK AND SUCCEED AT LIFE*

"There are books I endorse and books I endorse that I then ask my kids to read too. This is the latter. It took me until my midforties to learn the amazing lessons Tim teaches here. I'd love for my teenage daughters, friends, and family members to discover this Secret Society a lot sooner than that!"

—JON ACUFF, *NEW YORK TIMES* BESTSELLING AUTHOR

THE

SECRET SOCIETY

OF SUCCESS

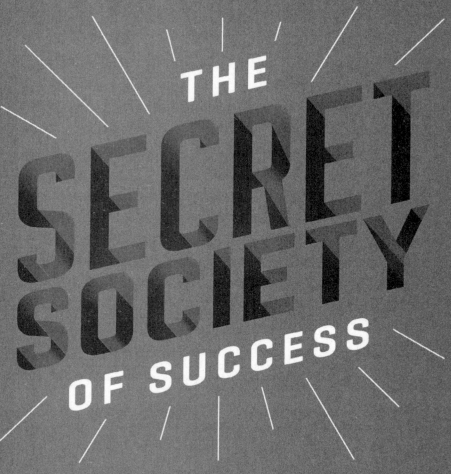

THE SECRET SOCIETY OF SUCCESS

STOP CHASING THE SPOTLIGHT AND LEARN TO ENJOY YOUR WORK (AND LIFE) AGAIN

TIM SCHURRER

NELSON
BOOKS

An Imprint of Thomas Nelson

The Secret Society of Success

© 2022 Tim Schurrer

Published in Nashville, Tennessee, by Nelson Books, an imprint of Thomas Nelson. Nelson Books and Thomas Nelson are registered trademarks of HarperCollins Christian Publishing, Inc.

The author is represented by Alive Literary Agency, www.aliveliterary.com.

Thomas Nelson titles may be purchased in bulk for educational, business, fundraising, or sales promotional use. For information, please e-mail SpecialMarkets@ThomasNelson.com.

ISBN: 978-1-4002-2944-4 (Audiobook)
ISBN: 978-1-4002-3771-5 (ITPE)

Library of Congress Cataloging-in-Publication Data

Names: Schurrer, Tim, 1986- author.
Title: The secret society of success: stop chasing the spotlight and learn to enjoy your work (and life) again / Tim Schurrer.
Description: Nashville, Tennessee: Nelson Books, [2022] | Summary: "Tim Schurrer, right-hand man to Donald Miller and executive director of StoryBrand, introduces readers to the Secret Society, a community of people who have learned a new way of defining success—where we stop chasing money, fame, and power and discover meaning and fulfillment in the work we do"—Provided by publisher.
Identifiers: LCCN 2021045166 (print) | LCCN 2021045167 (ebook) | ISBN 9781400229420 (hardcover) | ISBN 9781400229437 (ebook)
Subjects: LCSH: Success. | Successful people. | Conduct of life.
Classification: LCC BJ1611.2 .S335 2022 (print) | LCC BJ1611.2 (ebook) | DDC 158.1—dc23
LC record available at https://lccn.loc.gov/2021045166

Printed in the United States of America

22 23 24 25 LSC 10 9 8 7 6 5 4 3 2 1

To Judson and Elle:

May you learn to live in the way of the Secret Society.

CONTENTS

FOREWORD

Ten years ago, when I first started my company, I hired Tim Schurrer. We have built an eight-figure business together since then, and these days I think of Tim as the Billy Beane of business. What I mean by that is he's excellent at putting together a team and then creating an environment that fosters each person's specific skill set and passion so they can best contribute to the overall mission. He's good at building a team that knows how to win.

The key to Tim's magic is that last word: win. What does it really mean to win? For Tim, it wasn't only about the bottom line. It was also about people knowing the role they played on the team and striving for excellence together. It was about people feeling appreciated and valued and recognized for what they contribute. Tim believed the financial part of the business would take care of itself as long as you nurtured a winning team.

Tim and I certainly reviewed the numbers and had measurable

goals—goals that we hit. But what I noticed about Tim was that when a decision had to be made between hitting our goals and caring for our team, the team always came first. That makes sense. If you burn out your team to reach a goal, that will be the last goal that team reaches.

When I think about the growth of my company over the years, I see many challenges we had to overcome, but a strong company culture was never one of them. Because of Tim, my team was happy and focused and committed to one another as much as they were committed to excellence.

My years working with Tim taught me much, including that caring about the people you work with is as important or more important than the mission itself. A business will not grow unless the people who work in that business grow. I believe this to be true because I saw Tim do it and saw it work.

The Secret Society of Success, then, is all about building the kind of environment where people can grow. If you want to grow, or if you want your team to grow, some things may need to change, including how you define the very idea of success itself.

Sincerely,
Donald Miller
CEO, Business Made Simple and StoryBrand

THE
SUCCESS YOU'RE
LOOKING FOR

When you stop and think about the people who've had the great-est influence on our country the past one hundred years—through art, business, politics, sports—what names come to mind? Martin Luther King Jr.? Steve Jobs? Oprah? The Beatles? Barack Obama? Ruth Bader Ginsburg? Jeff Bezos? Tiger Woods?

These are the names that come to mind for most people. But what if I told you there's a whole group of people who have been just as influential, but you've never heard about?

What if I told you that *you* could be one of them?

This book will show you how to find true success, leave your mark on the world, and live a life of meaning—all without ever chasing recognition, money, fame, or power.

Don't get me wrong. There's nothing wrong with recognition, money, fame, or power. But are they reliable—or the only— indicators of success? It's time to challenge how success is defined.

– Is our only hope that, someday, we'll get our own "big break"?

– Do we have to make millions of dollars to say we "made it"?

– Should we spend our entire careers trying to impress, hustling for a raise or a promotion?

– Do our lives somehow mean less if we don't make it into the spotlight or to the top of the corporate ladder?

Intuitively we know these can't be the only markers of success, and yet, every day, many of us order our lives as if they were. We set our sights on the big raise or the next promotion or the new car or the million-dollar house. We hustle like crazy and pray we'll miraculously be discovered. We idolize celebrity and status and feel we haven't "made it" until our lives are admired like those in the spotlight.

And what is it giving us?

According to statistics, it's giving us anxiety, depression, frustration, and exhaustion.[1] The exact opposite of what we set out to find: success. But there's hope. We can shed some cultural misunderstandings about what success is and replace our current faulty definition of success with a better one. Not only can a new definition of success help us leave a lasting impact on the world, but it can also help us enjoy and find meaning in the work we are currently doing. We can have influence and a sense of fulfillment without any change in our current salary or platform. What I'm saying is this: you don't need a stage to make an impact; you need a change in mindset. And I'll help you make that mindset shift in the following pages.

For almost a decade, I was the right-hand man to *New York Times* bestselling author Donald Miller, running his company StoryBrand. I've been able to meet, talk with, and learn from so many different

people: from executives of billion-dollar brands to small business owners, from those who stand on stages in front of thousands to those
behind the scenes who organize the logistics at those same events.

Regardless of position or visibility, what has become clear to
me is that there are two kinds of people out there:

1. Those with a "Spotlight Mindset," who act as though
   recognition, money, fame, and power are the most
   important badges of success.
2. Members of the Secret Society, who have defined success
   in a different way.

This second group of people has captured my attention and
kept me asking question after question:

- If recognition, money, fame, and power aren't the
  endgame, what is?
- How does one live and operate in a world that values
  those things without bending to them?
- What are the *real* markers of success?

These are the kinds of questions we're going to dive into
throughout this book. But first we need to understand the cultural environment we're living in and how it contributes to the
Spotlight Mindset and our faulty definition of success.

WHAT'S IN IT FOR ME?

In business schools all over the world, students are being taught
to market to potential buyers from the stance of "What's in it

CHASING

SUCCESS

FOR

RECOGNITION

— OR —

NOTORIETY

IS *THE RECIPE* FOR A

MEANINGLESS LIFE.

TIM SCHURRER

@TIMSCHURRER / SECRETSOCIETYBOOK.COM

for me?" (WIIFM). Meaning, whenever they put together a marketing campaign for a product or a service, they're taught the focus needs to be targeted toward the customer's interests. What is it about the product or service that is going to benefit the customer and solve their problem? Whatever *it* is, focus on that in the marketing copy. Without WIIFM as the focus, no one would sell products and services in today's market.

But when it comes to building a career, a WIIFM attitude will kill your spirit and prevent you from making a meaningful contribution. In fact, my guess is that it already has.

Without knowing you at all, there's a reason I can feel relatively assured that you've been negatively influenced by the WIIFM culture we're all swimming in. It's not just because I've talked to hundreds of people just like you who are struggling to find satisfaction in their work. It's because this environment has been designed to influence you. The money is literally riding on it.

With the rise of commercialism, we are experiencing a rapid increase in the number of commercial messages we are exposed to. What was five hundred ads per day in the 1970s skyrocketed to as many as five thousand per day by the early 2000s.[2]

As consumers, we are being *bombarded* with an unprecedented number of commercial messages.

If that weren't enough, in Don's book *Building a StoryBrand*, he explains that one of the primary functions of the brain is to keep us alive.[3] It has learned to rewire itself and to conserve "calories" by ignoring information that does not help us to survive and thrive. And these days, knowing there's way too much information out there to process, our brains shut down if forced into information overload to keep us from red-lining.

To put it another way, the brain ignores information that's not written from the perspective of WIIFM. All that is to say: your brain is swimming in an environment that requires you to make decisions from this perspective—that is, unless you intentionally decide to do things differently.

It'd be ignorant to believe this brain rewiring is isolated to purchasing decisions. Quite the contrary. This consumer mindset is driving our behaviors in all areas of our lives. It's now our default mode to be thinking of ourselves constantly.

This default mode is not just a breeding ground for an unhealthy desire for attention and recognition. It feeds the Spotlight Mindset and keeps us dissatisfied with our lives—namely, chasing the recognition, money, fame, and power we're subconsciously craving.

It's a widespread problem, affecting even our youngest minds.

KIDS WANT TO BE YOUTUBE STARS

My friend Brad Montague is the man behind the YouTube phenomenon Kid President. If you haven't seen these videos, they star Robby Novak as a grade-school kid dressed up in a suit and offering bits of wisdom from the "Oval Office." The presidential seal in the backdrop of these videos may have been drawn on cardboard, but the words he delivers from that desk are nonetheless inspiring. Brad and Robby's first video, "A Pep Talk from Kid President to You," had over forty-five million views and launched them into the public eye.

Over the next seven years, they created hundreds of videos to inspire kids (and adults) to think differently about what's important in life. Their platform gave them a pretty large megaphone, getting the attention of President Barack Obama, Beyoncé, Tom Hanks, Steve Martin, and others they interviewed. It's safe to say the work they've done with Kid President has inspired millions.

Over the years, many people have reached out to Brad about Kid President, wanting to emulate its success. But more and more, he hears from a surprising population: kids. Are you curious to know the top question he gets? These kids want to know how they can become YouTube stars. They want to be *famous.*

Brad is one of the most humble people I know, and he doesn't crave attention. You see, he didn't create Kid President to get famous. He simply wanted to encourage kids with fun little videos. But then the videos started to spread and, well, they went viral. So when people ask Brad how they can become famous, he knows only one authentic response: "Don't think about the end result of what these videos will do for you as a creator, but instead get obsessed about the journey of making something that adds value to the world. Because if you want to be famous just for the success—the attention and recognition—then you've already missed the bigger picture. If you're only in it for yourself, you've got it wrong from the start."[4]

COUNTER TO WHAT CULTURE IS TELLING ME

If I were to listen to and act on what culture is telling me, I should be getting more credit for my work. I should have a bigger platform and spend more time up front and visible. More people should know my name. I should be making more money. I should be driving a nicer car. My house should be bigger. I should live in a better neighborhood. If only people knew what I was capable of, they'd finally show me the respect I deserve.

It's an easy narrative to buy into. If I'm honest, I've thought all these things and still do at times. But when I do, something just doesn't sit right.

On other days—and I would argue on my healthier days—I believe a little more humility and me slipping into the background is when I'm living my best life. I quietly do my work without thinking about who will recognize my contributions. I think of other people's needs before my own. And then I go home at the end of a workday grateful for everything I have, rather than in an endless pursuit for the things I don't. On my good days, I am comfortable giving away the credit, and success is a thing I have defined for myself, not something others have defined for me. Simply put: I'm at my best when I'm living in the way of the Secret Society.

I've learned that chasing success in its many forms for recognition or notoriety is the recipe for a meaningless life. My hope is that as you read through this book, you'll start to redefine success for yourself and notice when the Spotlight Mindset takes over. Stick with me, and I'll show you how to join a community of people—the Secret Society of Success—who have found the key to a fulfilling and impactful life and career.

I'll begin with a man who, literally and figuratively, embraced a life in the shadows.

DON'T AIM *at* SUCCESS — THE **MORE** YOU AIM AT IT AND MAKE IT A TARGET, THE **MORE YOU ARE GOING TO MISS IT** . . . **IT MUST ENSUE,** AND IT ONLY DOES SO AS **THE UNINTENDED SIDE-EFFECT** OF ONE'S DEDICATION TO A CAUSE **GREATER THAN ONESELF** . . . **IN THE LONG RUN—** IN THE **LONG RUN, I SAY!** **SUCCESS WILL FOLLOW YOU** PRECISELY BECAUSE YOU HAD *FORGOTTEN* TO **THINK ABOUT IT.**

VIKTOR FRANKL

THE

SECRET SOCIETY

"Houston, Tranquility Base here. The Eagle has landed."

With that, Neil Armstrong and Buzz Aldrin made their way from the lunar module *Eagle* to the moon's surface for the world's most famous walk. I'm sure you know the moment: "That's one small step for man, one giant leap for mankind." Can't you almost hear that echoey, old-timey voice playing in your head?

But what you may not remember is that there was another astronaut on Apollo 11 who isn't spoken of much. He'd just *ubered* Neil and Buzz to the moon but wouldn't be taking steps on it like his coworkers. Instead, he'd wait in space, orbiting the moon until they were ready to be picked up and brought back to earth. Not everyone could go down on that coveted walk. Someone had to stay with the Apollo command module.

That someone was Michael Collins.

ON THE DARK SIDE OF THE MOON

While Armstrong and Aldrin had the eyes and admiration of the world, Collins did laps around the moon. Twenty-six times, to be exact, while his partners completed various tasks on the moon's surface.[1]

In the shadow of Armstrong and Aldrin—indeed, in the shadow of the moon itself—Collins quietly did his job.

I like how one journalist clearly defined the stakes of Collins executing his role to perfection:

> Collins was under a different kind of pressure than the other astronauts: He was their only ride home. The crew would arrive at the moon together. Armstrong and Aldrin would travel to and from the surface in a lander, and Collins, in the command module, would release and recapture them. If something went wrong in these delicate maneuvers, the moonwalkers would be stranded. Collins needed to learn how to fly the command module back to Earth because there was a terrible chance he'd be the only one coming back.[2]

Needless to say, Collins's role was a crucial one. But he didn't quite touch the moon. He'd traveled 238,900 miles. He'd trained his entire career for the opportunity. He'd even been to space before and was uniquely positioned to be one of the chosen. Walking on the moon was one of the greatest accomplishments in history. And he missed it by *that* much. Not to mention, despite the undeniably famous "one small step for man . . ." echoing in your brain, you've probably never even heard Collins's name.

The president of the United States surprised Armstrong and Aldrin with a telephone call from the Oval Office while they were on the moon. Nixon spoke of the pride he and other Americans were feeling because of their historic feat, but he failed to mention Collins in his remarks. While the world praised the moonwalkers, Collins worked diligently in the shadows.

One thing I should share with you about Michael Collins, since you likely don't know much about him, is that he approached his work differently than most. Going to the moon isn't even the most impressive part of his story. More on that in a minute.

First, there's a reason I've brought up the moon landing.

Some of us are the Neil Armstrongs and Buzz Aldrins of the world: the ones who stand in the spotlight and garner a lot of attention, who make a significant impact on thousands (if not millions) of lives. It's hard to argue against the fact that some of us have been wildly successful in that kind of obvious sense. We're at the top, so it makes sense that others want to be like us and, therefore, we get a lot of attention.

But don't forget about the other kinds of success that are a little less in your face. Maybe we are more like Michael Collins than Neil or Buzz. No one knows our name. We're not necessarily making it big or getting widespread attention for what we do. Our role is important (maybe even vital) for our organization, but no one is mentioning us in their speeches.

Regardless of whether you're a Neil or a Buzz or a Michael, what I want you to see is that we need to both broaden and personalize our definition of success, or we risk going our whole lives feeling like we failed when we actually made history. We risk going our whole careers feeling like we missed the mark instead of understanding the truly vital role we played.

What we may not have realized until now is that we're all up against the same problem. While we may have varying levels of public attention, we're led to believe we should all want more.

More attention. More recognition. More money. More likes. More views on YouTube. A better version of our lives that's just beyond our grasp. The worst part is, this relentless pursuit for something we'll never attain is making us miserable.

What are we supposed to do about that?

LIVING IN YOUR DEFINITION OF SUCCESS

When most people hear the word *integrity*, they think of someone having good morals. Good values. Someone others can rely on. But there's a second definition: "internal consistency." And here's why I think that definition deserves some attention. Culture has sold us on the narrative, *"Get into the spotlight (whatever that looks like in your profession), and you'll have everything you ever wanted."* We're told this is "success." Culture is pushing you to get to the top at all costs. You know something's not quite right with that approach, but instead of identifying what's at the root of your unrest and then working to eliminate it, you keep on. The lack of integrity between who you want to be and how you are living is causing a rub. At the root of it, the reason you feel off is because you've been chasing after a definition of success that, deep down, you suspect won't make you happy. And yet you keep pushing, because you're not convinced there's another option.

Hey look, I've been there. I used to define success as owning a million-dollar house. There's a neighborhood a few minutes down the road from my house where I'll take friends who are visiting Nashville. When I say the neighborhood is crazy nice, that's an understatement. The cheapest house you can buy is a million dollars, but most of these mansions are between two and three million. I take people on a tour of this neighborhood with the same fervor as with other Nashville landmarks like the Ryman Auditorium and the Grand Ole Opry.

For a couple of weeks, I was really serious about wanting to own a house in my favorite neighborhood and would refresh my search constantly to see if any were up for sale. I wanted to picture my ten-year goal (or at least that's what I told myself). I wanted to dream of what my life could look like and what my friends would say about me as the owner of one of those houses.

It was actually quite fun to daydream about. And then one day I noticed myself feeling frustrated about the amount of money I was making, knowing I'd need a lot more to move into my dream house. The "if they only knew what I contribute" types of thoughts flooded my mind. Day by day my resentment grew, and slowly I found myself quite unhappy with my life.

After a little too long being sour, I had a brief moment of clarity. I started to think through exactly *why* I wanted one of those million-dollar houses. The justifications came flying in. *My kids would be set up in a better school district. We'd spend less money in the long-term because they could go to public schools. We love the area we live in, and this would only put us a mile down the road.*

These were all true. But if I were honest with myself, I knew none of these were the actual reason I wanted to move into that neighborhood. The real reason? I wanted to appear successful to my friends. If I had a million-dollar house, it'd show people that I was a person who had accomplished something and, therefore, that I was important.

It may be my constant desire to achieve or something else entirely, but sometimes doing a good job, working toward something meaningful, being part of a team, and serving the people around me don't feel like they're enough. Forget Michael Collins;

I want to be Neil Armstrong! I want to show those around me—especially the people I respect and think are accomplished—that I belong and can compete at the highest level.

But what do we actually need to compete at the highest level? That is the question that has been driving me ever since I read about Michael Collins. If what we need is the spotlight, then what does that say about the man who made the whole moon mission possible? Maybe there's a way to reevaluate our definition. Maybe we don't need a constant upgrade of houses or cars or followers to mark our success. Maybe we can track it with something different.

Here's a truth. The problem wasn't wanting a million-dollar house; the problem was my *intention* for wanting that million-dollar house. I was chasing a fantasy in an attempt to cover up a whole lot of internal dysfunction. I was relying on a fancy house to feel successful. And in doing so, I was not living with integrity. My internal consistency was off, and I could feel it.

I decided it would be best to delete my house-searching apps (I had downloaded three) and take a break. With a clearer head, I remembered what I had been missing the past couple of weeks during my million-dollar house search. Gratitude. I looked around my already-big-enough-and-beautiful home and my growing family. I had been so fixated on my big goal that it caused me to miss what was right in front of me, and it ultimately led me to resentment.

At my house, there's a pond out back. It's not a huge pond, but it's big enough to throw a paddleboard down from time to time. When my wife, Katie, and I were searching for our current house, we walked up the driveway and saw the water at the edge of the yard, and our jaws dropped. Even though we love the pond and the peaceful nature of it, it's easy to take for granted. Probably not unlike someone living in Colorado who no longer notices the mountains.

Staring at the pond and thinking about my two-week brain glitch, I realized I had gotten caught up in an unhealthy mindset. I listened to a world screaming more, more, more and completely gave in to the unhappiness of wanting to keep up with my peers.

You can probably relate to that feeling of wanting more, of being discontent, of getting distracted from the now by thinking of the next thing.

But imagine actually enjoying your life. Imagine taking breaks from the search for the next gig or the next position or the next company you want to start. Imagine settling into your role and being happy with the day-to-day. Imagine experiencing integrity and gratitude and rest.

What if I told you there are people out there who live their lives like this every day? Not only are they making a massive impact on the world, but they're deeply inspiring, competitive, magnetic people who would tell you they're living lives chock-full of meaning.

I mentioned them in the introduction, but it's important to know more about them so you can model your life in the way they live theirs. You, too, can join this Secret Society.

THE SECRET SOCIETY OF SUCCESS

The most impressive thing Michael Collins has done in his life, if you ask me, isn't the impossible mission that day with Armstrong and Aldrin. What he's done is live life according to his own definition of success. That is truly a miraculous feat.

What would make this a miserable story is if Michael Collins came back from his trip to the moon and acted like a victim. Can you imagine him trying to steal the spotlight away from the mission as a whole? "Yes, we made it back from the moon. But it sure would have been nice to touch the thing after all I went through." Given just how close he was, would anyone really blame him if he expressed just a little bit of resentment about not walking on the moon? It would be such a human response. But he didn't do that. Not even a little bit.

What's truly inspirational about Michael Collins is that he was solid in his definition of success. Collins recognized the value of his own position, he focused on doing his work with excellence, and he embraced his role, even when that didn't include having cameras pointed at him. "I was perfectly happy with the seat that I had, the part that I played in it. All three seats were required for mission success," said Collins, reflecting on his accomplishment.[3] The wisdom, maturity, self-confidence, and humility this requires is astounding. Collins was content with doing his job and doing it well. *That* is what he told the press.

The reward, here, was not the fame or the attention. It was the privilege of contributing to a larger mission, which is gifted to those who are willing to do the work. Somehow Collins became a man who didn't need the credit, who understood the larger purpose and everyone's contributions.

What if you took on the attitude and demeanor of Michael Collins, no matter how much attention you got? What if you accomplished great feats—made it to the moon, metaphorically speaking—but didn't put stock in whether the fanfare came with it?

This is counterintuitive, because most people would tell you the fastest way to success is to get into a position with more visibility. To be fair, I've known hundreds of humble, influential, world-changing people who have, in one way or another, been able to attain a considerable amount of visibility. And yet the ones I respect the most have something in common.

That something is an *attitude* à la Michael Collins.

They are people like James Higa, who some call "the Ninja" because of the stealthy tactics he used while helping Apple launch iTunes (among other top-secret projects). As the right hand to Steve Jobs, he worked for years taking meetings and making deals on Steve's behalf. There are stories of Higa taking freight elevators to meetings with record label executives to keep anyone from knowing Apple was creeping into the music space. Of course, Jobs needed someone he could count on, and he couldn't run Apple without some very competent and discreet people on his staff. Higa was one of those people for him, a role Higa defined as "special ops."[4] While he was one of the most influential people on Apple's staff and in the office of the CEO, Higa kept undercover so he could serve his boss and company with excellence. One of his friends told me, "He spent ten years becoming invisible to make Steve great."

Here's another hugely influential person who doesn't get much airtime: Viola Spolin. While you may not have heard her name before, I imagine you've heard of *Saturday Night Live*.

While serving as a drama supervisor in the 1930s and 1940s, Spolin encouraged actors to focus on the present moment and improvise as though they were functioning in real life, instead of simply speaking rehearsed lines from memory. This was something she called "theater games."[5]

Several years later, Spolin's son would open a theater called The Second City in Chicago. With the help of his mother, he applied theater games to improvisational theater, and this magical blend created what we know today as improv comedy. Over the past forty years, The Second City has been the breeding ground for actors looking to make it big on *SNL*.

There would be no world of modern improv, no Second City, and certainly no *SNL* if it were not for the work of Viola Spolin. It's also likely these Second City and *SNL* alumni would not have become household names: Steve Carell, Stephen Colbert, Tina Fey, Amy Poehler, Joan Rivers, Martin Short, Bonnie Hunt, Julia Louis-Dreyfus, Chris Farley, and Bill Murray. Still, you probably hadn't ever heard of Spolin.

What do Collins, Higa, and Spolin have in common? Well, they weren't restlessly searching for the next big thing. They simply embraced (and thrived in) their roles and, as a result, made a huge impact in their industries.

They are part of this secret society of people who define success in a different way. These people do not need attention or recognition to survive. They work hard, they contribute to major achievements, and they support others without their ego getting in the way.

If you want to be part of the Secret Society of Success, you have to learn to think and act differently than most. I'll share stories of its members with you, and I hope they will inspire you as much as they have inspired me. My life is infinitely better because I follow their lead.

Being a member of the Secret Society of Success looks like this:

- You define success for yourself and live into that fully.
- You find a deep sense of fulfillment in your work, but that sense of fulfillment does not depend heavily on recognition or external validation.
- You help others win.

- You are among the hardest-working people in business, full of ambition.
- You make the people around you and the projects you contribute to better.
- You can thrive in the spotlight but also don't mind being behind the scenes.
- You are servant-minded and purpose-driven.
- You are more interested in what you can do for others than what they can do for you.*

It sounds so simple, right? And yet so few people are willing to do the work to adopt this way of life. But if you do, it will shift your paradigm and have you living in a completely new way.

The picture of success the world gives us is selfish. And yet it's natural. We come into the world kicking and screaming and thinking of our own needs. We cry until we are fed. We demand what we want until we get it. But as we become adults, we won't find fulfillment until we learn how to think about others, offer a meaningful contribution, and make life about more than just ourselves.

GETTING BACK ON TRACK

The way I define success has changed over the years—in fact, quite drastically. I've already told you about my dream of a million-dollar house. There was also a season in my life when I was dead set on being the next John Mayer (I'll tell you *that* story later). For me, success is no longer fame. It's not a title or a salary.

---

* For a daily reminder to live in the way of the Secret Society, visit SecretSocietyBonus.com, download the poster, and hang it on your wall.

LIVING IN THE WAY OF THE SECRET SOCIETY

Redefine Success

Help Others ⤳Win⤳

STOP CHASING *the* *SPOTLIGHT*

SUCCESS IS <u>IN THE</u> ASSIST

Focus on the process

RECOGNIZE OTHERS

ONE LIFE AT A TIME

WHO AM I HERE FOR?

Be a FIREFIGHTER

DON'T MIND WHO GETS THE CREDIT

You don't need a stage

SERVE OTHERS

It's not constant recognition. And it's not a house in a specific neighborhood. Success is living in the way of the Secret Society, no matter the situation I find myself in.

Adopting the mindset of the Secret Society isn't easy, and no one is perfect at handling it. Even those who have worked at this for a long time may oscillate from day to day. I'm sure Michael Collins didn't have the healthiest mindset every minute of every day while on the Apollo 11 mission.

I, too, can get off course. I don't think at every moment, *I'm super content. I don't need anyone to know how much I contributed here.* The reality is that sometimes I think, *I wish I got a little more credit for my work.* But then I get the smelling salts from some of my mentors who have taught me how to live in the way of the Secret Society.

When I get more on track living in that way, I'm more at peace. And I'm grateful for my life, rather than constantly looking for what's missing from it. Wouldn't it be great if you could spend more time feeling content and fulfilled?

It's possible, and I can show you how. But it won't come without a fight. We have a major challenger: the Spotlight Mindset.

I THINK EVERYBODY
—
SHOULD GET
RICH AND FAMOUS
AND DO EVERYTHING
THEY EVER DREAMED OF
SO THEY CAN SEE
THAT IT'S NOT
—
THE ANSWER.

JIM CARREY

2

THE

SPOTLIGHT MINDSET

Years ago, I was having lunch with my friend Andrew. We sat down at one of our favorite burrito spots in Nashville and were doing what we always do, talking about life and work and what was going on with both of our families. At one point in the conversation, when things were getting a little more serious, Andrew leaned in and confessed, "I think I'm trying to be someone I'm not."

Sobered, I nodded for him to go on.

When Andrew was sixteen, he went to a concert and was awestruck. At that moment, he thought, *I gotta do that.* And pretty quickly, he said, "I was on a mission to become the person on that stage."

Fifteen years into his journey as a musician, he had reached the end of his rope. He was constantly comparing himself to others, and he felt like no matter what he did, he wasn't experiencing the kind of success he knew was possible in his career.

At this point he had been sober for over a decade, so I knew he was spiraling when he said this next thing: "Either I'm going to start drinking again or something has to change. These panic attacks are putting me in a place in my mind where I'm losing it. There are moments when I think I'm gonna die."

Surprisingly, this came at a time when you'd have thought things couldn't be better for him. On the outside, it looked like he had all green lights. He was on a headlining tour and selling hundreds of tickets a night. He was supported by a management team, booking agent, and record label. He had a beautiful wife and was beloved by his friends.

On the inside, though, he was in a tailspin, caught in a comparison trap. No matter who he compared himself to, he wasn't living up to that image. No matter what chart he was on, he wasn't where he felt he needed to be, and he was paying for it with every part of his life. He wasn't present at home with his wife. He was losing sleep. The stress and anxiety were more than he could bear at times, and he knew that wasn't any way to live. "I need to do something opposite of what I am doing. I am hanging on by a thread and starting to think this isn't life. I'd rather be in a different profession and not have to keep up with this thing anymore," he said. What had started as a dream had trapped him.

Here's what's crazy. It hadn't always been this way for Andrew. There was a time in his life when music wasn't all about comparison. There was a time when music was a passion for him. It was an outlet. It was his sanctuary. His escape.

From the time he was a kid, Andrew wanted to be a musician. After the concert he had experienced as a teenager, he had known that's the kind of magic he wanted to make. After years of work, he was finally a career musician. So how did it turn him into the person he didn't want to be?

THE MINDSET THAT'S HOLDING US BACK

To have the attitude and perspective of Michael Collins is counter-cultural. It's counterintuitive. The way of the Secret Society is not what we do naturally.

Our default is what I call the Spotlight Mindset. This mindset tells us the only thing that matters is attention, praise, notoriety, fame, and titles. This is the mindset that tells us we won't be happy until [fill in the blank]. Until we get our big break. Until we have more followers. Until that video gets more views and comments. Until we get our big promotion. Until. Until. Until. This mindset has the potential to ruin our lives. We have to learn to identify it and then work to fight against it, or it will start to take over.

A simple definition for the Spotlight Mindset is this: *an unhealthy desire for attention and recognition.* And it's getting in the way of the kind of success that brings about fulfillment in our lives and careers.

Where does this mindset come from? Well, everywhere. We see the Spotlight Mindset in the culture at large in a million ways.

You can see it in the way people use social media, curating successful images of themselves, in the way the influencer culture has taken off, and in the obsession with becoming a verified account. It's as though you're not important unless you're perceived to be; therefore, you strive for a particular way to brand yourself to get more followers and likes.

You can see it in game shows and contests: everyone looking for their fifteen minutes of fame, their way to be at the top quickly. It's fostered by shows like *American Idol*, *The Voice*, and *Master Chef*—the idea that you have greatness in you; you just haven't been discovered yet. A Spotlight Mindset says to do whatever is necessary to get into the center of the narrative and show the world how talented and successful you really are (or can be).

It's in people's attitudes: always hustling for more, never being content in their current situation. It's in the idea that you have to become the boss or start your own company if you really want to be somebody. It's in the restlessness we feel to always be on the move or to show others how much control we have over our own success. It's in the idea that you can skip several steps and experience immediate success and, along with that, gain respect and admiration from others.

The Spotlight Mindset manifests in different ways for every person, and there are plenty of ways this mindset wreaks havoc. Here are the seven major symptoms of someone trapped in a Spotlight Mindset:

1. **Striving.** Do you struggle to find contentment in your life? Does it lead you on a restless pursuit for more?
2. **Comparison.** Do you wish you were someone else or wonder how your success stacks up against others? Are you jealous in a way that gets in your way?
3. **Damaged relationships.** Does money, fame, or status trump other things in your life? Are your relationships suffering because of it?
4. **Fear of failure.** Do you believe a successful life and career should be a stress-free journey to the top? And if failure or struggle were a part of the story, do you worry about your image as someone who didn't always win?
5. **Seeking validation.** Do you feel unsatisfied until someone else acknowledges and approves of your work?

6. **Selfishness.** Are you so laser-focused on your own success that you forget to be a champion for others? Do you invest any of your time in service of someone else's goals, even if it has nothing to do with advancing yours?

7. **Seeking influence.** Do you believe you need a bigger stage to have a life of significance?

As you read through that list, what stood out to you? Is there one symptom (or maybe a couple) that you can identify in your own life? Maybe you brag to your friends and family about your salary. That's the Spotlight Mindset in action. Maybe you name-drop to get someone's attention or admiration. That's the Spotlight Mindset. Maybe you go back to your hometown to see old friends and find yourself wanting to really impress them, so you brag about the cool projects you're working on. A flex of the ego. One person trying to become greater than another. That's the Spotlight Mindset.

I was walking through an airport a couple of years ago, and I heard a young woman say to her friend, "I just want to be famous." Her friend asked, "What would your platform be?" She threw back her head and said, "I don't even care."

And that's the truth. Most people don't care how they get there or why. They simply want the end result. They desperately want the impressive title, the assistant, a little more attention and recognition. The ability to walk into a room and have instant trust and credibility. For people to think they're important. But they don't know what contribution they'd like to make in the world. They don't know who they are or why they matter.

I'd like to warn you: the Spotlight Mindset leads us anywhere but to success.

STUCK IN A HOLE

Without constant self-awareness, I, too, can slip into the Spotlight Mindset. For several years our company was part of an association made up of businesses in our industry. The association hosted an annual conference where we'd go to learn from keynote speakers and to connect and share best practices with one another.

The people who hosted the conference organized breakout groups according to company revenue. The logic was that people in a similar revenue group probably experience similar challenges. For example, the founders of companies with less than a million dollars in revenue are probably trying to duplicate themselves and struggling with the adage "Growth or control, choose one." Those with $20 million companies, though, are thinking about completely different things. They are likely struggling to reinvent themselves and looking to innovate with new products and services. Their challenge may also be in getting their various teams to collaborate more effectively.

While this type of sorting makes sense conceptually, throughout the conference I felt like my company's revenue was on my name tag:

HELLO

TIM SCHURRER
StoryBrand
[Company Revenue]

I also felt like that's how I was treated—that is, according to my revenue. Year after year, as we attended this conference, I had a desire to be in a higher-revenue breakout group. I found that a company created a buzz within that community if they grew in revenue quickly, and I wanted to gain everyone's respect.

Well, we were fortunate to have had fairly rapid growth a few years in a row, and it began to happen. I was gaining respect from people every year. (At least, that's how it felt to me.) It was intoxicating and I began to crave it. I knew this wasn't healthy, because it's as though my motivation to be with these bigger companies was less about having the ability to learn from them and more about the opportunity I had to (secretly) look down on the lower-revenue companies from my pedestal.

Suddenly my identity was wrapped up in my company's revenue. I will say, though, this wasn't playing out externally. My problem was happening internally, in the posture of my heart and mind. I was trapped in the Spotlight Mindset.

I caught myself doing this again, in a different way, last week. I was talking with my grandma, of all people, and I guess I wanted to impress her. I found myself bragging about how my company has grown and the number of people we had on staff. Why did I feel the need to talk about that? Well, I wanted her to think my life is interesting and, therefore, think more highly of me. (Which is ridiculous.)

Before my dad passed, I remember telling him about the opportunities I had been given at work, because it almost felt like if I was involved in projects with major brands, he would be more proud of me. (Which is a lie.)

For many of us, it's easy to find ourselves striving for a little more attention and recognition.

Maybe you find yourself at the end of your rope, jealous and stressed and overcome with comparison fatigue. Or maybe you feel lost, wondering where your life is headed. Or, perhaps, like most of us, you're exhausted. You're tired of the climb to get to the top, and you have nothing left to give. Whatever motivated you to start the climb isn't cutting it anymore. If you're honest, you don't recognize yourself some days. This is not the life you set out to create for yourself.

But, more often than not, the Spotlight Mindset will tug at you far more gently. It starts whispering its lies when someone close to you succeeds, when you start to feel dissatisfied, or perhaps with the allure of that next promotion or better job. You may not notice it at first, but then you start to experience its negative effects. If you live in that space for too long, it actually distracts you from the kind of impact you could be making.

The Spotlight Mindset all too easily creates an underlying feeling of restlessness, of striving, of discontent. It's the feeling of being in a hole and not knowing how to get out.

At least that's what it's been like for me.

LIVING IN THE TENSION

As much as I want there to be one, there's no magic fix in all of this. No silver bullet. Fighting the Spotlight Mindset is not something we can check off a list and move on from. It's a daily struggle.

The Spotlight Mindset will ruin your life if you let it. But let's stop looking at it as a problem that can be solved, something that can be fixed permanently. Instead, I want you to recognize it for what it truly is: a tension to manage. It's not ambition or contentment. It's both. It's not recognition or flying under the radar. It's both.

A few years ago, my friend Tim Arnold released a terrific book, *The Power of Healthy Tension*, to help explain this "living in a tension" paradigm.[1] To get the 101 on understanding tensions, breathing is a good teacher. We're constantly inhaling and exhaling. If all we did was inhale, we couldn't survive. Tensions are like that. It's not an either-or; it's a both-and. To be at our best, we've got to live in the tension between the push and pull, the inhales and exhales of life.

There are tensions all around us, and the biggest mistake we can make is to believe we can solve them. Tim observed that the second you swing to one side and try to correct your problem, you'll find you've mismanaged the other. Again, these are not problems to solve; they are tensions to manage. It's not bad to get the promotion or even to want the promotion. In fact, healthy things grow. Which means that when you're healthy, your success will naturally grow. You won't have to force it or make it happen. It's not bad to be the boss or the team lead. I'm not saying throw out your ambition. Let me be clear: ambition is a great quality to have. It's the unhealthy desire for those positions or for the affirmation that comes from a title that will derail your life.

The key here is the word *unhealthy*. Remember how I told you I wanted a million-dollar house? There is nothing wrong with owning a million-dollar house or having the kind of money to afford one. Those homes and neighborhoods are full of wonderful people who are doing important work. What was wrong was my obsession with it, my feeling that having that kind of home would change the way others felt about me and my success.

There is also nothing wrong with wanting recognition.

THE *SPOTLIGHT* *MINDSET*
WILL DISTRACT YOU FROM THE
KIND OF IMPACT
YOU COULD BE MAKING.

TIM SCHURRER

@TIMSCHURRER / SECRETSOCIETYBOOK.COM

Wanting to be acknowledged comes from a good place. We all want our lives to mean something.

I have some comforting news for you: the way of the Secret Society is the path to having the kind of impact you desire in your life and career. You don't have to give that up. (Though you may define *impact* a bit differently by the time you finish this book.) As far as wanting more recognition than you're getting? We'll deal with that in a few chapters.

Throughout this book, we're going to approach *the Spotlight Mindset* and *the way of the Secret Society* for what it is—namely, a tension to manage. We can strive to live in the way of the Secret Society, but we will find ourselves at the other end of the spectrum at times. Living in this new way will require practice. You don't wake up one day and achieve it. In fact, there's no finish line on this one. What I want to do is help you recognize the Spotlight Mindset in yourself and give you some tools to transcend to a better way of thinking and living.

These tools come in the form of mindset and paradigm shifts—in new ways of looking at people, situations, and ourselves. It's all in our perception. We'll fight an unhealthy mindset with a healthy one. As you get to know the way of the Secret Society, you'll start to notice the people around you who are living in this way. You'll see them at work. You'll see them *everywhere*.

The stakes couldn't be higher. For Andrew, having a Spotlight Mindset could have cost him his life. I'm not trying to be over-dramatic. I am simply pointing out how much this stuff matters. Having the tools versus not having them could be the difference between having anxiety and panic attacks, wasted years of discontent, day after day at work without enjoyment or any amount of enthusiasm, sleepless nights, and tension in relationships—or not.

All this because we don't have the right mindset about how

to define success? It seems like such a simple thing, and yet the ripple effect of getting this right will make a difference for you and everyone in your orbit: your friends, your family, your co-workers, and your community.

How, then, do we avoid the Spotlight Mindset and live the life we were designed to live?

A LADDER TO CLIMB OUT

Andrew's story started with a dream, a passion. But fifteen years into that pursuit, he was not experiencing the dream. He didn't feel like he was "making it." No matter how hard he tried, he was striving to write the next hit, to get new fans, to become a star. And it was destroying him. "I am so deep in desperation to become known and seen and relevant that I am literally in panic. My body can't take it anymore. My heart is restless. I am having trouble sleeping. I can't keep up with this dream that I thought I was supposed to become," he told me.

At this low point, he made a drastic decision (out of necessity really) to walk away from his dream. He started to accept the reality that he'd never write and record another song or go on another tour. He needed to learn a new approach to life, because the way he was living was heading toward a major crash.

It's been several years now since that lunch at Baja Burrito with Andrew. And, by the grace of God, anxiety and panic and desperation don't describe his life today. He's a completely different person, and just talking to him feels different now. He went on a journey to discover who he really wanted to be, and it brought him freedom.

What's crazy is that this path led him back to his dream. "I'm slowly stepping back into music," he reflected at another one of our lunches not too long ago. The difference this time is that he's not letting success define him. "It was the willingness to explore who I was without music that gave me perspective. Freedom isn't found in reaching goals and dreams. It's found in letting them go to make room for new ones."

Andrew has found a new motivation for his career in music, a new way to define success. He's no longer in it for recognition. He's no longer trying to force something or trying to be someone he's not. And his mental health is in a whole new place.

Can you think of an area of your life where you're restless and not at peace? Most of us can. It might not be about a career like Andrew. But maybe you have experienced a similar feeling at some point. Perhaps you're feeling that no matter how hard you work, you'll never live up to the expectations you have for yourself. Maybe you feel like you're constantly trying to impress people and it's not working. And maybe, like Andrew, you feel it is affecting your mental health.

No matter who you are, life can be tough. It's draining. It's full of times when other people have what you want and may even get the credit and recognition you deserve, and you need some help along the way.

In the following chapters I'm going to equip you with the tools you need to fight against the Spotlight Mindset. I have learned all these lessons from members of the Secret Society, and they flat-out work. I will introduce them to you, so that whenever you are stuck in a hole, these tools will be the ladders you need to climb out. And with some practice, you'll learn to climb even faster.

ASK NOT

WHAT YOUR TEAMMATES

CAN DO FOR YOU;

— ASK WHAT —

YOU CAN DO

FOR YOUR

TEAMMATES.

MAGIC JOHNSON

3

SUCCESS IS IN THE ASSIST

At the end of an unprecedented season in 2020, LeBron James and the Los Angeles Lakers won the NBA Finals in an unprecedented fashion.

As was true with much of the sports world, the National Basketball Association (NBA) was at risk of not being able to finish the season. The NBA's commissioner, Adam Silver, shocked the world with his announcement on March 11, 2020, that the NBA would be on hiatus for a minimum of thirty days. The courage of Silver and his colleagues to make that decision was the domino that tipped the rest. Shortly after, the PGA Tour, the National Hockey League, and all the other major sports leagues announced COVID-19 shutdowns as well. Not only that, the NCAA's flagship basketball tournament, March Madness, was also canceled.

We didn't know the duration of the hiatus for the NBA or

other organizations in the sports world at the time, but it would be months before it would be safe to play again. A world without sports was a pretty big shift and shook many to the reality of what would be a historic period in our lifetime.

The NBA worked around the clock, buried deep in the logistics of health and safety protocols, to find a safe way to start up again. No plan was without risk, and even with the best strategy, there were variables that would have been impossible to consider on the front side. COVID was a different kind of beast, and in the early months of the pandemic, it wasn't clear if getting takeout for dinner could expose you to the virus, let alone playing a game of basketball.

But after 141 days of an indefinite hold, the NBA kicked back in, thanks to Disney World. Yes, you read that correctly. The NBA set up a bubble in Orlando at the ESPN Wide World of Sports campus to close out the regular season and then wrap things up with an end-of-year playoff series we'll hopefully never have to experience again. The playoffs didn't start until September (they typically start in April). Then, on October 11, after knocking off the Portland Trailblazers, the Houston Rockets, and the Denver Nuggets, the Los Angeles Lakers were in a position to win the NBA Finals.

The Lakers showed up in game six of the Finals and defeated the Miami Heat to win the championship, 106–93. In that game, LeBron logged a triple-double with twenty-eight points, fourteen rebounds, and ten assists. When the craziest season in NBA history came to a close, it was LeBron and the Lakers who took home the trophy as the NBA's best team.

There's another trophy given out every season to the scoring leader, the player in the NBA with the highest points-per-game average. It's a big deal to be the scoring leader—Michael Jordan won the title a record-setting ten times. Few would argue that LeBron is also one of the all-time greats and has all the talent in the world to win that scoring title.

But do you know what I think is most interesting? In 2020, he didn't win the scoring title. He wasn't even in the top five. He was the leader in something else. That year, LeBron James led the NBA in *assists*. Meaning, the way he chose to play was to involve his teammates and for them to win together. Not for him to take over games and fly solo.

If that's not an example of the way of the Secret Society, I don't know what is.

NOT "WHY AM I HERE?" BUT "WHO AM I HERE FOR?"

The most successful people I know make the people around them better. They're all about the assist. It's not intuitive. You'd think that success would come by setting *yourself* up for success.

For most of my early career, I was definitely focused on setting myself up to win. That meant pursuing the degree that made sense for me, getting a good job at a reputable company, and then focusing on my individual performance to make sure I was the top candidate for the next title or promotion. It seemed to me this was simply the way of the world: everyone looking out for themselves. And so that's what I did too.

My quest to be successful consumed me. During college and in the years that followed, I often asked myself, *Why am I here? What I meant by that was, What should I do with my life? What can I do that will bring me the success I want? What will give me the greatest impact?* I was looking for purpose, a career, something to do that was meaningful, something that fit me. But mostly I was looking for a magic solution: some position or line of work that would launch my success.

Recently I've begun to ask myself a new question.

In 2017, I had the privilege of hearing author and leadership expert Andy Stanley address a crowd about purpose and career at a business conference in Atlanta. He explicitly called out "Why am I here?" as the wrong question.

We've been trained (by commercialism, by advertisements, by institutions) that the world revolves around us. Products and services are positioned as tools to make our lives better or give us something we don't already have. Asking "What's in it for me?" time and time again has the potential to lead us to the Spotlight Mindset, which is a dangerous path to be on.

But there's another question we can ask to get us into a better headspace, one postured in the way of the assist. And that question, Andy Stanley said, is "Who am I here for?" This question wakes us up from the self-centered environment we're living in. It pulls us out of the noise and into a more holistic view of life. What is all of this about? Who does my work impact? How can what I do every day serve others?

As I said before, helping others win can feel counterintuitive. You might be wondering, *Won't I jeopardize my own success by helping others win?*

In setting the team up for success, LeBron gets to experience even greater success for himself. When his team wins, he wins too. The reality is that personal success often comes as a byproduct of supporting others. That said, it's best not to have a Spotlight Mindset—namely, the idea that we will assist others only if it's the path for us to ultimately get ahead. Serving alongside others shouldn't be a manipulative tactic. We have to redefine our view of success more holistically, that even serving alongside people beyond your immediate team or company is a win for humanity. By showing up with your best effort and assisting others, you can't lose.

Focusing on other people's success is the way to achieve all the success that you want and are looking for—that is, if you begin to define success in the way of the Secret Society, where individual success doesn't mean as much as team success.

From my perspective, Andy Stanley and LeBron James have parallel messages. They are coming from different contexts, but they are both holding up the same idea: when you make the people around you better, that's when you truly win.

A TEAM VIEW OF SUCCESS

For those who live according to the Secret Society, winning is always about the team. Depending on where you're at in your career or what kind of role you have, having a team view of success will play out in different ways. Let's take a look at a few examples.

My friend Bob Goff was a highly successful lawyer for more than twenty-five years. Bob lives in San Diego, but before he quit his practice, he commuted to his office in Seattle, where he and his firm specialized in construction defect cases. If the windows of a high-rise started falling out or if the building was tipping over, Bob would figure out who was responsible. These were massive lawsuits worth millions of dollars, and Bob has never lost a case.

To say Bob was successful as an attorney would be an understatement. But it's not his winning percentage or the amount he settled from those cases (over half a billion, if you're wondering)

THE MOST SUCCESSFUL PEOPLE I KNOW MAKE THE PEOPLE AROUND THEM _BETTER_. THEY'RE ALL ABOUT THE ASSIST.

TIM SCHURRER

that made him a success in my mind. What makes him a success is how much he's been able to help others.

Bob told me, "When I found who was responsible in these defect cases, it was like a bunch of rich people throwing money at each other. And then the lawyers were standing in the middle, collecting it all. So, I just thought, 'You know what? I think I got more gears. I think that there's more here for me.'"

He was on a trip to India when he saw little girls, who were his daughter's age, being bought and sold into sex trafficking. And it felt personal. It wasn't like he was seeing this happen to somebody else's daughter; it felt like it was happening to *his* daughter. And he decided, "I just don't want to take notes or make observations anymore. I want to make a difference. I don't want to just agree. I want to actually get involved, get some skin in the game."

These days Bob is known as an influential author and speaker. He's written several bestselling books, including one of my favorites, *Love Does*.[1] Love Does is also the name of the nonprofit he started. The work began in 2002, not only to help those girls in India be freed from sex slavery but also to provide a safe place for them to live and recover from their trauma.

As far as funding? Bob decided the more money he could make as a lawyer, the more money he could put in to this organization. That's right. For over a decade, while he was winning case after case, he was doing something else quietly and under the radar. He was supporting a cause he cared about. He was making wins not just for his clients but for children across the globe.

Over the years, Love Does has expanded. What started as one safe house became two. Then they built a school for children in Uganda after finding out education was one of the biggest problems for these kids. Then they built another school. And another. Some of these schools and safe houses are in the most dangerous areas in the world. To visit some of these places, Bob and his team have to wear bulletproof vests and surround themselves with armed guards. But that doesn't stop them from investing in the lives of those kids.

This work with Love Does was so fulfilling that Bob began to see his law practice merely as fundraising. Can you imagine? You're running one of the most successful law firms in the Pacific Northwest, but you don't allow yourself to get too wrapped up in it. In fact, you win these massive cases and use the money to build schools around the world and help children escape from the abuse of sex trafficking.

It would have been easy to get head faked by the success of the law firm. If people had known Bob was spending his free time building schools and safe houses on the other side of the world, they would have ridiculed him for not staying focused and doubling down on growing his firm. Hire more people. Take on more cases. Expand beyond California and the Pacific Northwest. Pocket more cash.

But Bob viewed success a bit differently than most. He wasn't too concerned about his status or how others perceived him. What got him up every morning was the idea that he could make an impact in someone else's life who didn't have the same opportunities he had. He wanted to be of service to these kids and give them a new start in life. "Success is something that has a really long shelf life," he told me. "With the years I've got left, I just want to do stuff that'll actually last."

There was a morning when he got off at the twenty-fourth floor of the Washington Mutual Tower and walked into his office, and the receptionist asked, "Hi, who are you here to see?" He'd been spending so much time overseas that, even though Bob's name was on the wall behind her desk, she didn't recognize him.

He hadn't been to his office in over a year. He knew then it was probably time to call it quits and give even more of his time to Love Does. And so that's what he did.

My point is, although Bob is now a fairly well-known name and someone who has generated a lot of revenue for his business, he doesn't define his success in that way. His success has come from the way he's chosen to serve others and from his desire to help others win.

ERADICATING HOMELESSNESS TOGETHER

Dan Heath is the author of *Upstream*.[2] In his book, he related the account of Rockford, Illinois, which became the first city in the United States to solve veteran and chronic homelessness.

Homelessness is a complex issue. It has several root causes, including systemic injustice, child abuse, mental illness, and much more. So how did they tackle it? Larry Morrissey, the mayor at the time, knew he couldn't solve the problem alone. With a problem as big as homelessness, he was going to need an army to make a dent.

What Larry decided was that, as a politician, he had a unique ability to gather together various organizations: social workers, the police force, nonprofit organizations, and religious organizations. While there was no way he could fly solo on this one, he knew if he worked to serve the people who could solve this problem, they could make progress together. Before this, with all these various organizations working separately, nine years had passed with no progress at all in the city's goal to eradicate homelessness. Then, within nine months, they finally did it.

With all hands on deck, they took a person-by-person

approach: naming each individual who was homeless, gathering intel from each organization about them, and, one by one, finding them housing.

For Larry, the answer to "Who am I here for?" included the veteran and chronically homeless population.

In my life, I apply this principle in a more modest way than Bob or Larry. Maybe you can too. For me, it's reminding myself of my team. Since the time I listened to Andy's keynote address, I've had a fresh pair of eyes to look at my work, and I decided I'd show up for my coworkers. They are the people I serve. In my office, I created and hung an 8½ × 11 poster with the names and photos of every team member and their families.* At the top, in big, bold letters, I wrote "Who Am I Here For?" as a daily reminder of why I choose to bring my best effort and resist the Spotlight Mindset.

You know how it goes on any given morning. As you arrive at your office and start taking steps toward the front door, your mind is flooded with all the tasks you are about to jump into, your list of meetings, and that you have to leave work right at 5:00 p.m. to make it home in time for your routine of dinner and sports practice shuttling and homework with the kids.

I've tried to implement a new habit in these moments. As I'm walking toward the office door, I try to spend even thirty seconds thinking about a single question: *All right, Tim, who are we showing up for today?* And while that doesn't make my list of meetings any shorter and doesn't reduce the number of tasks I have to complete, the shift in perspective ushers me into a new posture for the day. I find myself slowing down and having my antenna up for the ways I can be of help to the people I

---

* To download a template of this poster that you can customize and hang in your office, visit SecretSocietyBonus.com.

interact with. Sometimes I'll see someone looking or sounding overwhelmed and have the presence of mind to offer support, or I'm able to mirror the excitement another person is showing up with.

The alternative is to worry only about myself and beeline it to my desk to start getting my work done. There's a time for that, don't get me wrong. But the pace I want to have in my work and the mindset I want to walk in with each day is not one of hurry but of connection and care for the people I'm spending each day with. I want to have the assist top of mind.

THE DOMESTIQUE

Even if you're not into cycling, chances are you've heard of the Tour de France. You can likely picture those men on their bikes, hunched over their handlebars, whizzing downhill at speeds up to forty miles an hour. It's incredible to see.

What I didn't know until recently is that there's a team of people, including other cyclists, who sacrifice to help a single person on their team—the lead cyclist—win that day's portion of the race (the race consists of twenty-one daylong stages over twenty-three days). They give a yellow jersey to the rider who crosses the finish line first.

Domestiques are cyclists who sacrifice their chances of being the star (the yellow jersey) by helping others. They'll pass around water to teammates and often ride out in the front of the pack to block the wind for the team. If there's an accident or bike malfunction, domestiques will sometimes even give up their bikes. So, for every guy who puts on the yellow jersey, it wasn't in any way a solo effort.

NASCAR has a similar system: pit crews change a tire or refuel as quickly as possible so their driver can win the race.

But the cycling example is even more poignant because the yellow jersey and the domestiques are both out there riding together. Domestiques are talented cyclists too. They have to be some of the best and able to keep up or even lead the pace from the front of the pack, all while caring for the others on the team, addressing challenges, and helping them succeed.

The question I have for domestiques is this: Why? What is motivating you? They are professional cyclists. At one point, they probably wanted to win the Tour de France, to be the one in the yellow jersey. But they've decided to play a different role. Do you think they're happy? I guess that all depends on how they view success.

Let me ask you this: Would you be happy as a domestique, or would you need the yellow jersey to feel successful? However you answer that question says a lot about what your attitude is and where you may still need to do some work.

I have the same question for James Higa, who, you know, worked alongside Steve Jobs for so long: Why were you willing to be invisible? What motivated you to sacrifice your own recognition for the sake of somebody else? What drove you to do this?

I think Daniel Pink, who wrote the book *Drive*, would say there's a whole other kind of motivation these people are operating from: an intrinsic sense of motivation.[3] They have an internal drive to help not just themselves but also to help others succeed. These people have embraced the truth that the success of the team is better than, and more important than, individual success. They have found their part, their role in the larger whole.

You don't have to wear the yellow jersey to be successful. You can be a domestique. You can quietly serve your team.

And when you do that, you get something even better than the spotlight. You get to wake up every day content with what you brought to the table. You resisted the urge to make it all about you and, instead, used your talents to help someone else win. The sense of fulfillment that brings is more satisfying than any amount of recognition you could ever receive.

IN THE SPOTLIGHT BUT PART OF
THE SECRET SOCIETY

You might be reading this and wondering, *Can I wear the yellow jersey and also be someone who serves others?* Maybe you are already in the spotlight in some way or have plans to be. Maybe you want to win the Tour de France. Is there anything wrong with having the drive to accomplish something like that? Of course not. You can be in the spotlight and still have an attitude of service. In fact, when you bring an attitude of service to a position of leadership or influence, it makes you twice as powerful.

Let's talk about LeBron James again for a minute. He is in the spotlight. In fact, he couldn't be *more* in the spotlight. As one of the most well-known athletes in history, he has all the traditional markers of success that society tells us to chase: money, fame, power. But his actions reveal an underlying attitude that he's oriented his life around helping others and helping the team as a whole. And it's not just in basketball where he's all about the assist.

The LeBron James Family Foundation supports students who are at risk of falling behind academically and could very likely slip through the cracks.[4] The foundation had been serving kids in LeBron's hometown of Akron, Ohio, for years through their

I Promise Program, but they leveled up their commitment in the summer of 2018 when they opened the I Promise School in partnership with the Akron public school district.[5] The students in the I Promise School are those who placed at the bottom of the list in academic performance in the Akron public school system and have a history of behavioral problems. These kids are in desperate need of help if they are going to have any chance of graduating from high school. Thousands of students have been impacted over the years by the work of LeBron and his family's foundation. They've leveraged their influence to ensure these kids are successful in school and in other parts of their lives.

Bob Goff is in the spotlight too. He's sold millions of copies of his books and has used his success as an author and a lawyer to create opportunities for others, not to build himself a taller fence. The work with his nonprofit Love Does has expanded, and it is now in seven countries: Afghanistan, Congo, India, Iraq, Nepal, Somalia, and Uganda. And if I had to guess, it won't stop there.

What I hope you're starting to see is that the way of the Secret Society has very little to do with your position or visibility. It has much more to do with how you hold yourself, how you view your career, how you support others, and whether or not you're willing to drop what the culture around you screams about success and actually do the work of defining it for yourself.

So, no, not everyone in the spotlight operates out of the Spotlight Mindset. And I assure you not everyone who plays a role behind the scenes is part of the Secret Society. The way of the Secret Society is available to us all, regardless of our position. But it's up to you to decide the approach you'll take in your life. Will you abandon the all-too-common Spotlight Mindset for the entry into the Secret Society?

WHEN NO ONE HAS YOUR BACK

Years ago, an application came through for a job we posted at StoryBrand, and the applicant had one of my favorite brands listed on their résumé. I was excited and curious to hear more about their experience working there.

Surely it was an incredible place to work. It had to be. Their products were amazing. The company was massive and had revenue in the billions. They were doing something right and had been for decades.

But I'll never forget what the applicant said during one of the early interviews. When I asked what it was like to work for this massive company, they said, "It's a group of really competitive people, but no one there has your back."

"What do you mean no one there has your back?" I asked.

They went on to explain that the team members were focused on themselves and their next position. Their priority was to ensure they were set up for the next promotion, and they would do whatever was needed to make sure nothing got in their way. Not even their own team members.

That was sad for me to hear. I had built up this brand in my mind and assumed they could do no wrong. But they violated one of the primary rules of the Secret Society—"Help others win"— and it was costing them. Their culture has been taking a hit, and they are losing top talent.

You might be thinking, *But their revenue is in the billions. It's hard to argue they're not successful.* On the revenue and brand side, sure. But who cares about all that when their employees don't support one another?

If I circled up the cofounders of this company and told them their team members don't have one another's backs, I'd be curious to know what they'd say. If they are saddened to hear about this, they are likely members of the Secret Society. If they're not, and instead point to their revenue as the measure of their success, they're still learning what it means to define success in the same way we do.

As a business, nothing is more important than a team. Truly. The team is all you have. A brand is a group of people, and these people make the products the brand creates. Their interactions with the brand's fans and customers are what create the customer experience. The sales of each product come from a salesperson, or from a marketing campaign put together by a team of people. In fact, even the website where the purchase is made is created by a team of web developers.

A team approach to business is what makes the whole thing work, which is why it was so crushing to hear that colleagues feel like no one has their back. This company's leadership has allowed the most important part of running a business to slip under their watch. What a tragedy.

It's not the competitive part of their culture that's problematic; it's the *way* they're competitive. So worried about individual promotion or opportunity that their team members are willing to tear one another down to get it.

Nobody there has your back. That is never said of anyone in the Secret Society.

SUCCESS EXACTLY WHERE YOU ARE NOW

What would it mean for your life and career if you asked the question, "Who am I here for?" What would it mean for you to be the person who passes the ball? What would it mean for you to have a team view of success instead of an individual one?

No matter your position on the org chart, try to create opportunities where you are benefiting others.

When I feel the Spotlight Mindset coming on, when I'm tempted to push forward too hard, when I start to feel resentful of other people's success, I ask myself, *Who am I here for?* This question changes everything. Asking this question opens you up to new possibilities, reengages you in the work you're already doing, and helps you see just how much you have to contribute. This approach suddenly infuses all kinds of meaning and purpose into your job, whether you're a domestique or a yellow jersey.

The way of the Secret Society is to lean toward the team-success end of the spectrum. Our default, the Spotlight Mindset, will pull us back toward individualist thinking if we let it. It's like gravity in that it has a way of pulling us downhill. But what if we learned to continually push against gravity and spend a little more energy on the team-success side?

At the summit, you'll find the "Who am I here for?" way of thinking. And if you give that more airtime, I argue you'll be happier and more fulfilled with the job you have right now.

The way of the Secret Society teaches us to be on a team—to compete *with* each other, not against. Your success is my success, and our success together is greater than what I could accomplish on my own. Success is helping the people around you get better.

Success asks, "Who am I here for?"

Success is in the assist.

SUCCESS

DOESN'T

HAVE <u>TO</u> COME

AT SOMEONE ELSE'S

EXPENSE.

DAVID HORNIK

4

PLAYING BY THE WRONG SCOREBOARD

As a kid, I loved going to the grocery store with my mom to look at the lobsters. They were in a tank at the very back of the store, right next to rows of iced fish. Before I pressed my face to the glass of the lobster tank, I'd reach up and grab a few pellets of ice that the fish were lying in and put them in my mouth. I made sure not to grab the stuff right up against the fish, but, still, I'd sneak it or my mom would give me that "that is so gross" look while shaking her head and trying not to laugh. (Let's agree: this *was* so gross.)

After my little ice snack, I'd watch the lobsters for a bit. They always had rubber bands around their claws, which I imagined were to keep the customers safe if they ever had the courage to reach in and touch one. I was way too afraid to try something like that.

Little did I know the rubber bands aren't for the customers (most of whom aren't dumb enough to stick their hands in the tank), but for the lobsters themselves. Turns out, lobsters are in a constant battle for dominance and are willing to fight one another for it. In fact, much of their survival depends on who's on top.

When they're not living in grocery store tanks, lobsters can be found on the ocean floor. In the book *12 Rules for Life*, Jordan B. Peterson explained:

> They need a home base down there, a range within which they hunt for prey and scavenge around for stray edible bits and pieces of whatever rains down from the continual chaos of carnage and death far above. They want somewhere secure, where the hunting and the gathering is good. They want a home.[1]

In Lobster Land, as is true in thriving cities, a good plot of land is hard to find. And so lobsters do what humans do when they spot valuable property: they leverage their power and resources to take control of it.

Like I said, lobsters are willing to fight one another to prove their dominance. When they're competing for territory, it starts with them going at each other without any real contact at first. Mainly they just strut at each other until someone backs down. But if that doesn't happen, strutting turns into a wrestling match, with one trying to flip over and pin the other. If they can't settle it in *that* round, they go at each other with their claws open wide, and "once a body part has been successfully grabbed, the grabber will tail-flick backwards, sharply, with claw clamped firmly shut, and try to tear it off."[2] Yikes.

Regardless of how many rounds it takes for this battle to escalate, there's a clear winner and a clear loser. Not only does the winner get the prized house, but the dominance hierarchy

PLAYING BY THE WRONG SCOREBOARD | 49

has been established and there's no confusion about who has the power.

Winning in Lobster Land has other benefits as well in that this powerful victor is very attractive to females. During mating season, they flock to the dominant male in hopes of getting some of his sperm.

Dominant male lobsters have it all: the house, the women, the power.

SCOREBOARDS ARE ALL AROUND US

It's not difficult to see the resemblance between our culture and Lobster Land: both are obsessed with certain metrics of success. I like to call these "scoreboards." For lobsters, the scoreboard tallies the number of other lobsters that one male dominates and the position he gets from it. For us, scoreboards tally money, status, or influence.

It's not hard to find scoreboards. Just look around. Get online or open an app. You'll find stats and rankings according to myriad different systems: games won, money made, number of views, units sold. The list goes on.

More often than not, we buy in. We rank ourselves according to the number of followers and likes. We're constantly measuring ourselves against others—and therefore, our perceived dominance—by the car we drive, the neighborhood we live in, our title or salary, the schools our kids attend, or who best keeps up with the latest fashions and trends. We're led to believe that whoever is at the top has all the power and gets all the attention.

The truth is this: scoreboards are hard to escape. They are in the natural world, demonstrated by those lobsters, and they're all around us in society.

They are even built into our biology. It's more natural to search for power and status than not. Another way to say that is: we're hardwired to rank ourselves according to scoreboards. As Caroline Zink, a neuroscientist at the National Institute of Mental Health, observed, the hierarchies we live in "are a strong determinant of social behavior and have enormous impact on health in humans and other primates."[3]

In a study led by Zink, participants were asked to play a computer game and were told they'd be scored based on their response time.[4] They would be asked to press a button "when a blue circle changed to green" or "to indicate the box with more dots." When they responded fast enough, they'd get a dollar.

The participants were given time to practice before the session began. One of the participants was then told they had been given a rating as a two-star player. It was also explained that the two other participants were given ratings as a one-star player (worse) and a three-star player (better) based on their practice sessions. Keep in mind these players had not seen each other up to this point. As this information was revealed, they were shown pictures of the other two players and functional magnetic resonance imaging (fMRI) was used to measure brain activation.

Viewing the three-star player activated an area called the occipital parietal cortex, which processes attention, and the ventral striatum, which is involved in rewards. This suggested the participants paid attention to and valued the higher-ranked player more than the lower-ranked player.

But here's the catch: the one-star and three-star players didn't exist. The participants' responses were based on an arbitrary rating alongside fictional characters. And yet the participants gravitated toward the one above them on the scoreboard. They wanted something the three-star player had—namely, a higher status.

What's also interesting is that, in the original instructions, the participants were told they weren't competing against the other players and that their scores wouldn't affect one another. "Despite the game being non-competitive with the other players, participants were strongly engaged in the hierarchical context, as evident by post-session questionnaire data."[5] Meaning, we engage in these hierarchies subconsciously, even when there are no real stakes.

Not only are scoreboards out there, but they are also *in here*, woven into our biology. We are hardwired to believe that success means getting to the top. So to minimize the facts about the hardwiring of hierarchies or to pretend these scoreboards don't exist would be disingenuous to our actual lives.

Whether through the company org chart or comparing follower counts on social media, dominance hierarchies shape our lives. The battle for power is all around us, and we're in it whether we realize it or not. We have more in common with lobsters than we'd like to admit.

But is that all that's possible for us, or can we be more than lobsters?

SCOREBOARDS CAN'T RANK HAPPINESS

The Spotlight Mindset tells us to demand attention and find a way to get to the top of whatever scoreboard we can. Even though the pull of hierarchy is hardwired in us, I believe it's distracting us from where we actually want to go.

Harvard launched a study in 1938 in the midst of the Great

Depression.[6] They pulled together 268 Harvard sophomores and a group of boys from what were considered Boston's poorest neighborhoods and began studying everything about them.

What's become the world's longest study of adult life has a primary aim: to learn what makes people happy.

With over 2,500 people participating in the study year after year, the researchers comb through thousands of data points looking for trends. They dig deep into mental health, physical health, work, and relationships. They're curious to know how these factors impact happiness as the participants progress through adolescence, through their teenage years, as young adults entering the workforce, as some become parents, as seasoned professionals, in the later years of their careers, and finally as they age and experience retirement.

Some of the early participants are now in their nineties, which gives researchers a unique opportunity to look back in a way very few studies can. What the data has revealed after all these years is that "close relationships, more than money or fame, are what keep people happy throughout their lives."[7]

It's not that surprising of a discovery, but it's contrary to what culture is selling. Marketers everywhere are busy offering you *things* when the thing that will make you happy is already within reach.

Not only this, the stress caused by living within dominance and social hierarchies is negatively affecting our mental and physical health. Studies show that anxiety about status can lead to cardiovascular disease and weakened immune systems, among other health problems.[8] The more we fixate on status, the more problems we experience.

And yet the Harvard study revealed something we all know to be true: "Good relationships keep us happier and healthier."[9]

We have some lobster tendencies, and we live in a lobster society, but we are not lobsters. Although they are great at competing with each other, lobsters do not experience the full range of human emotions, such as joy, sadness, or adoration. Most importantly, they don't live lives of meaning. But we have the option to do so. We can live like a lobster and fixate about our position on scoreboards, or we can evolve beyond our most basic instincts and experience the richness of life in relationship with others. Only then can we find true happiness and success.

I have personally found this to be true.

BUT I WAS SUPPOSED TO BE JOHN MAYER

When I was eighteen, I wrote my first song. It wasn't very good, but that didn't stop me from dreaming about what my life as a famous musician would look like. I could see the path before my eyes, and I was sure I was going to become the next John Mayer.

Over the next few years, I wrote a few dozen songs, recorded them, and even released a couple of CDs. Seeing my albums on iTunes was pretty surreal. With my music now available for everyone to hear and a hairdo that'd make even Steven Tyler jealous, I was sure the world would know my name before long.

As you may have guessed, that didn't happen.

After my mom and her friends bought their share, I was left with boxes and boxes of my CDs stacked in the garage without a clue as to how to get them into people's hands.

I couldn't get people to show up at my concerts in Kansas City (where I grew up and was living at the time), and my Myspace stream stats were dismal. It was frustrating, because no matter how hard I worked, I wasn't seeing the progress I wanted. Until I found a way to sell more records and get my stream numbers up, it was unlikely I'd ever get asked to be an opening act on a larger tour. And with that opening slot being my gateway to success (or so I thought), I needed to figure something out.

In hopes of improving my chances of being discovered, I packed my things and moved to Nashville for my junior year of college. I went to Belmont University, which was full of aspiring musicians just like me.

While I was struggling to get people to listen to my music, I noticed that wasn't the case for other artists I was building friendships with.

There was a guy at Belmont named Steve Moakler, and it was annoying how good of a musician he was. So many of my friends asked, "Have you heard the new Steve Moakler songs?" They were talking like *he* was the next John Mayer, which was impossible, because *I* was going to be the next John Mayer. Yes, I had heard his new songs, but I didn't want to like them. The guy was writing stuff I wish I had come up with and had a pop sensibility that was surely going to land him on the radio.

Not only that, he was a good-looking guy who could have been mistaken as one of the Jonas brothers, with his dark, curly hair. And he was nice too. So annoying.

It took me a couple of months, but I turned the corner and finally admitted to myself and others how good Steve's songs were. Knowing how many people listened to his songs on Myspace every day, I knew he had a national fan base, and I thought if I could tour with him, it would expose his fans to my music and get me a step closer to my dream. This was the opportunity I had been looking for. I needed a tour concept for the two of us, and then I needed to pitch him on this big idea.

While I didn't have relationships with any music venues, I

wondered if people would host us in their backyards. I had a portable sound system, which was loud enough for us to play to well over a hundred people. The typical person may not have hosted a house show before, but it's something I knew we could help them figure out. Simply put: if they had ever invited friends over to their house for a barbecue, they could host a house show. They'd provide the friends and the lawn, and we'd bring the show to them.

The planning and the logistics this kind of tour required came easily to me, so if Steve was up for the house show idea, I knew we'd be able to pull it off.

I saw Steve in the Belmont cafeteria later that spring and decided to pitch my tour concept. I needed him to say yes, because without him on the bill, I was afraid I'd miss my chance to perform in front of new fans that summer.

I nervously approached him, introduced myself, and explained my idea of these house shows. He was engaging and approachable, and our conversation, even as complete strangers, was very natural. I was thrilled to learn that he had never been on a tour like this before and was really into it. I got my answer: he was in.

After some planning in the days that followed, we landed on a tour name—The Home Is Where the Heart Is Tour—and started promoting it to everyone we knew. Within a couple of weeks, we had put together a nice run of shows, primarily through the Midwest, which is where the majority of Steve's fans were at the time.

That summer we played ten shows in eleven days, traveling around in Steve's Honda Element with our mutual friend Jamie, who was taking pictures and documenting the tour to share with our fans on Myspace.

During the first week of the tour, we had cruised through Indiana, Ohio, and Michigan and were on our way to Illinois for a couple of shows in the Chicago area. I was in the back seat with my thoughts while Steve and Jamie alternated between casual conversation and freestyle rapping in the front. I was thinking about how hard I had worked to become a musician compared to how easily I had planned this tour, and what might change for me if I wasn't actually going to be the next John Mayer.

We were several shows into the tour by now, and at this point I was a big fan of Steve's songs and of him as a person. But I couldn't shake the jealousy I felt when I saw how people engaged with him and his music. He sold three or four times as much merchandise as I did every night, and every night people were singing along to his lyrics. It's like he wasn't even trying and people loved him. When someone bought a CD from him and not from me, it felt like rejection.

Comparison is hard to deal with at any point in your life, but especially in your early twenties when you're still trying to figure out who you are.

At this stage, I defined success as becoming famous and more liked than my peers. And I was struggling because Steve was getting so much attention, and it felt like I was losing. But was it even a competition? The scoreboards (i.e., number of fans and amount of merchandise sold) were real. But what about the meaning I was giving them? Was that real or just a figment of my imagination?

Either way, here's what I knew: it was stealing my joy. One might say I was being a lobster, or at least living by Lobster Land rules.

Fortunately for me, this wasn't the end of my story. I realized I could find success in other ways—ways that came naturally to me and didn't require that I become famous. But before I could do that, I had to lay down my Spotlight Mindset. I'll tell you more about how I did that as this book unfolds.

Perhaps you, too, have felt the all-consuming pull of the scoreboards around you. Guess what? They will always be there. We have to learn to live with a healthy mindset in the midst of them or we're toast. It's critical, then, for us to find a new approach.

There's no question something in us wants to have power and status. But that's not the best part of us. The best part of us wants to find meaning and accomplish all that's possible for us in this life. The question is this: When we're living in Lobster Land, is it possible to be any other way?

CHOOSING COLLABORATION OVER COMPETITION

It was late September, and the Seattle Seahawks were in town to play the Tennessee Titans. At the time, my friend Ben Malcolmson was the right hand to Pete Carroll, head coach of the Seahawks. Ben invited me and a small group of friends to a closed practice on Saturday afternoon where the Seahawks would do a walk-through of all the plays they had been working on that week in preparation for the game the next day.

These are the invitations I don't pass up. Seeing Coach Carroll, Russell Wilson, Doug Baldwin, Richard Sherman and the Legion of Boom from the sidelines was going to be quite an experience. Thank goodness the practice field was inside, because the weather that day was typical of late September in Nashville: sunny, in the upper eighties, and with enough humidity to make you sweat while standing still.

There was only one rule at the practice: no pictures or videos. What we were about to see were the actual plays the Seahawks were going to run against the Titans, and they couldn't risk them being seen in advance if anything were to leak on the internet.

Three charter buses rolled up, and the players and coaches stepped off one by one. They wandered onto the field, and then, as soon as everyone was inside, a whistle blew and the players moved into their appropriate positions. This cadence of a whistle followed by the players running into a precise formation lasted for about forty-five minutes. The offense, defense, and special teams ran through their plays (including trick plays), and then a final whistle brought everyone into a huddle to officially bring the walk-through to a close.

Immediately after that last whistle, Ben and Coach Carroll jogged over to the sideline to say hello. After a few minutes of casual conversation and a picture of our group with Coach by the team photographer, the two joined the rest of the team and headed toward the buses.

As quickly as everyone had arrived, they were gone, and we were left standing on the sideline of an empty practice field.

And it hit me.

One hundred thirty guys had traveled from Seattle to Nashville for this game, and only sixty of them were players. That means seventy people were at the practice that day to contribute to the team from the sidelines. They would never set foot on the playing field during the game on Sunday, but that didn't mean they were any less motivated to work hard. The coaches, equipment managers, security agents, trainers, and doctors, all give everything they have throughout the season to help the eleven guys on the field compete at the highest level.

The support staff of a successful team like the Seahawks take an approach to life that most people don't: instead of obsessing about their rank or status, they focus on what they can bring to support others. It's a "Who am I here for?" approach. The relational bonds forged in this kind of culture can't be overstated.

Keeping our eyes glued on society's scoreboards will leave us feeling exhausted as we grasp at the next rung on the ladder. Over time we learn that reaching the next rung doesn't get us what we wanted. The kind of success that will leave us satisfied will only come in relationship with others.

Lobsters don't seem interested in helping others, and the scoreboards we see in our lives (sometimes by the minute) tend to pit us against everyone else. But when we choose collaboration over competition, dominance and social hierarchies don't matter much.

EVOLVING PAST "IT'S ABOUT ME"

We come out of the womb, and from the very beginning, the story is about us. When we cry, there is someone on call to give us whatever we need. We get so much attention, even our siblings roll their eyes.

As we become toddlers, a common phrase is "The toy is *mine*!" and we are quick to melt down if anyone tries to tell us otherwise. At this point in our lives, we've not learned much about caring for others.

As we age, this mindset sometimes stays with us, and the saga continues into adulthood. But it comes out a little differently. "The toy is *mine*!" (i.e., "It's all about me!") looks like everything we've talked about in this book so far: Clawing our way to the top, even if that means stepping on others along the way. Doing whatever it takes to get the year-end bonus, even if it's at the expense of our customers. Covering up our mistakes to shine a better light on our performance.

But we don't have to continue in this way. "It's all about me" is a natural stage of human development, but it's possible to evolve beyond it.

OUR WIRING TELLS US *to*
FOCUS ON OURSELVES
—— AND ——
DEMAND ATTENTION
WHILE THE SMALL, QUIET VOICE
DEEP INSIDE US SAYS
THERE'S POWER IN SERVING
ALONGSIDE SOMEONE ELSE
and HELPING THEM
REACH THEIR POTENTIAL.

TIM SCHURRER

In Adam Grant's book *Give and Take*, he defines two kinds of people: givers and takers. He described these two contrasting types in the workplace:

> Givers are a relatively rare breed. They tilt reciprocity in the other direction, preferring to give more than they get. Whereas takers tend to be self-focused, evaluating what other people can offer them, givers are other-focused, paying more attention to what other people need from them. These preferences aren't about money: givers and takers aren't distinguished by how much they donate to charity or the compensation that they command from their employers. Rather, givers and takers differ in their attitudes and actions toward other people. If you're a taker, you help others strategically, when the benefits to you outweigh the personal costs. If you're a giver, you might use a different cost-benefit analysis: you help whenever the benefits to others exceed the personal costs. Alternatively, you might not think about the personal costs at all, helping others without expecting anything in return. If you're a giver at work, you simply strive to be generous in sharing your time, energy, knowledge, skills, ideas, and connections with other people who can benefit from them.[10]

When we're so focused on competition, it can feel like being a taker is the only way to succeed. But that's simply not true. There is a group of people who focus on others, and it ends up being good for them in the long run. Grant argued:

> Most of life isn't zero-sum, and on balance, people who choose giving as their primary reciprocity style end up reaping rewards. . . . It takes time for givers to build goodwill and trust,

but eventually, they establish reputations and relationships that enhance their success.[11]

We know how important relationships are to our happiness. Everyone loves a giver because they try to make people's lives better and use their resources and connections to help others win. The support staff on the sidelines for the Seahawks? Givers. They are helping the players perform at their best.

Lobster Land is all about takers (whoever is at the top and has the power wins), and it's an easy one to get sucked into. But I'm not buying it. We don't have to be at the top to survive. In fact, our happiness has nothing to do with our position. If we're constantly thinking about the scoreboard and obsessing on where we rank, we're sunk.

This is where a lot of us get tripped up. Our wiring tells us to focus on ourselves and demand attention, while the small, quiet voice deep inside us says there's power in serving alongside someone else and helping them reach their potential.

We can't pretend hierarchies don't exist. They will always exist. In life, you will come up against these scoreboards, and they will entreat you to return to the Spotlight Mindset. Scoreboards remind us that competition is the way of society at large, but we have to remember that they don't lead to happiness.

While we might not be able to leave our own Lobster Land, we are not lobsters. And while we are wired for hierarchy, we are even more wired for relationships. A fulfilling life is available to us, but not until we give these scoreboards less of our focus.

What you'll learn as you start to progress in the way of the Secret Society might surprise you: you don't have to beat anybody to win.

WE ALL WANT
TO BE SEEN,
WE ALL WANT TO KNOW THAT
WE MATTER.
AND THE MOST YOU CAN
EVER DO FOR SOMEBODY IS
TO SHOW UP
& ALLOW THEM TO KNOW THAT
THEY HAVE BEEN
SEEN AND HEARD
BY YOU.

OPRAH WINFREY

5

LOOKING FOR
A LITTLE BIT OF
RECOGNITION

One of my favorite places to watch a concert is the historic Ryman Auditorium, which is not too far from where I live in Nashville. Recently I was there to see one of my favorite artists. I sat on one of the pews in the balcony, just a few rows away from the stained glass windows that line the back of the auditorium.

At one point during the show, the lead singer moved from standing center stage with a guitar to the piano. This transition to the piano placed him a bit farther back and, for just a couple of seconds, the guy running the spotlight lost him. The spotlight seemed to be doing figure eights in the middle of the stage, and it was clear to everyone the guy was struggling.

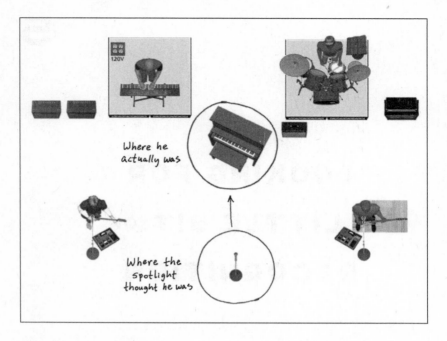

The lead singer called him out—"Gotta stay with me, bro"—in a kind, joking way. The audience laughed and the show went on. But I couldn't stop thinking about what had just happened.

If the musician and lighting guy had been in sync, no one in the audience would have thought about the guy running the spotlight or known he was there. But because of a single mistake, he captured everyone's attention—the attention that was supposed to stay center stage.

Isn't it interesting that if the lighting guy did his job well, night after night, no one would notice? Even though his job is crucial to the success of the evening, he is, more or less, invisible.

THE RECOGNITION YOU DESERVE

Do you ever feel invisible? Do you feel like no matter how hard you work, how excellent your work is, how important your role is, that nobody fully understands the depth and breadth of what you do?

Here's a truth that may be hard to swallow but is important nonetheless: no matter how much you do, how excellent your work is, and how important your role is, you will likely never be fully recognized.

This applies to all of us, regardless of our position within a company. First, I think of people who carry the weight of leading a team. Take the president of the United States, for example. I've heard it said that POTUS only deals with the most difficult situations or problems, because if there were an easy resolution, someone else would have already solved it before it got to the president's desk. For leaders, this comes with the territory, but that doesn't make it any easier to manage.

Most people won't ever fully understand the stress of having a back-to-back schedule of putting out fires. Having the stress of cash-flow management, knowing that any mistake made on your watch could mean the difference in a person on your team (and sometimes their family) having a paycheck to pay their rent and put food on their table. It's a lot to handle, and yet so much goes unnoticed.

Second, I think of the majority of people who play a supporting role on a team. Their role is different from their boss's, but to them it feels no less stressful. Most companies don't have the problem of being overstaffed, and therefore the number of hats team members wear can feel overwhelming. Perhaps budget cuts reduced the amount of people on your team, and now you're expected to deliver the same results with three people when you used to have six. There are more spinning plates than ever before, and a lot of this goes unnoticed while you work long hours just to keep up with the endless cycle of deadlines.

Regardless of your role on the team, most people don't fully understand all that you do day after day. This leads to a lack of recognition, because how can someone recognize you for something they don't know you did? It's a cycle. There's so much work that happens in your role that other people don't fully understand, you're not recognized for it, and then, in time, you may start to question your value.

UNDERSTOOD ⟶ RECOGNIZED ⟶ VALUED

And guess what happens when you don't feel valued? Over time the passion for your job evaporates or burnout arises, and you start looking for what's next. Even if you loved your job at one point, that passion isn't sustainable through the grind of stressful days when you feel underappreciated.

You're not crazy for feeling this way. To want recognition is not weakness, it's human. We talked about Lobster Land in the last chapter and how our biology, as well as culture, is wired to want attention and be at the top of various hierarchies. The same is true for recognition. It's ingrained in us to want to be recognized. It's coming from a good place. Who doesn't want to feel valued? Oprah Winfrey wrote,

> In all of my talks and understandings over the years, doing thousands and thousands of shows, I came away with the understanding that the thread that runs through all of our human experience is that we all want to be validated. We all want to be seen, we all want to know that we matter. And the

most you can ever do for somebody is to show up and allow them to know that they have been seen and heard by you.[1]

The need for recognition is hardwired into each of us, regardless of our position or the amount of visibility we have in our roles. But the problem isn't simply that we want to be recognized. That can be a good and healthy desire. The problem arises when that good desire overtakes our lives in an unhealthy way. This is the Spotlight Mindset at work.

When we don't feel seen by people we work with, the Spotlight Mindset starts whispering its lies. A simple thought—such as, *you're not getting the recognition you deserve*—repeated over and over, can lead us to an unhealthy headspace, causing us to react from resentment or frustration that's been building inside of us. We may not even know the resentment is there until we see the symptoms of the Spotlight Mindset in action. And this can happen to anyone. It's just as easy for a team member as it is for the CEO to pat themselves on the back in front of the team to make sure no one forgets what they bring to the table. When we start demanding the attention and recognition we think we deserve, it not only distracts us from making any progress toward our career goals but keeps us from feeling fulfilled.

The truth is this: you may not get the recognition you deserve for the work you do. How you respond in those moments is what differentiates those in the Secret Society.

THE RECOGNITION GAP

In reality, we're not looking for much. A simple "thank you" from the right people for the work we do actually goes a long way. In fact, we know that we're not asking for much, which makes it all the worse that we don't feel seen.

It's true that the act of recognition is simple. And yet most people are not good at it. It's not because we're bad people. We're just busy with all we have to manage and likely feel we're doing a better job of giving it than we actually are.

Think about how much recognition you get (or don't get) from your boss. Unfortunately, as much as everyone wants to be acknowledged by their boss, the nature of a manager's role—and the nature of yours—works against this. They are managing several people and projects and simply do not know how much goes into your job. They are thinking about other tasks, and noticing your efforts and all that you're juggling is not top of mind.

To make matters worse for those behind the scenes, managers often have an overinflated view of how much recognition they give to their direct reports. Dan Heath, author of *The Power of Moments*, addressed this when he was a guest on the StoryBrand podcast. He told us,

> There's this great study that shows if you ask managers, "Do you frequently recognize your direct reports for the work they've done and honor them for that work?" eighty percent of them say, "Yeah, I do that." And then if you ask their direct reports, "Do your managers frequently recognize you for the work you've done?" twenty percent of them say yes. So we call that the "recognition gap."[2]

Those of you in leadership harbor similar feelings. When you do your job well, things run smoothly and the details of everything you're doing go overlooked.

Expecting your peers, direct reports, or leaders to give you recognition sets everyone up to fail, both you and them. You're setting yourself up for failure because you are putting hope in something that is unlikely to happen. And it sets others up for failure because you're holding them to a standard they likely won't deliver on. (The stats I just gave you from Dan Heath are proof of this.)

So when it comes to addressing feelings of going unseen, you have to stop looking exclusively to others.

CREATE A CULTURE OF RECOGNITION

If looking to others isn't going to work, there's only one person left to make a change: you. The Secret Society is full of people who take it upon themselves to initiate and encourage a culture of recognition.

Let's start with a small, highly achievable action item, something I like to call shout-outs.

For years, my friend Sarah Sloyan was the senior vice president of EntreLeadership, a division under the Dave Ramsey umbrella that equips business owners to become better leaders. When she was running the business, I would always try to spend as much time as possible with their team, because when I did, I'd leave with a couple of pages of notes and a list of things we could implement at StoryBrand to make our team better.

Sarah invited me to one of their weekly stand-ups (staff meetings), and from the start I knew it was going to be a fun meeting. You could feel the energy in the room, and it was clear that everyone wanted to be there. Everyone seemed to be smiling.

The meeting followed a predetermined agenda, updating the fifty or so staff standing in a circle about what was important to know for the coming week. Near the end, they celebrated their new customers by hitting a bell for each product that was sold, with genuine excitement.

For the closing section, they opened the floor for shout-outs, where the team could recognize their peers for going above and beyond. The week leading up to the meeting, they had wrapped up a significant update for one of their digital products, so a developer got a shout-out for pushing out the latest changes to their customers. A few others received verbal pats on the back and the meeting wrapped on a high note.

As the staff headed back to their desks, I caught myself day-dreaming, thinking through how we could mimic this recognition piece at StoryBrand. With minimal effort, Sarah and her team had just boosted the energy of the entire room by shining a spot-light on what could have easily gone unnoticed. A website change could be seen as pretty basic, as the developer simply doing their job. But not on this team. They recognize excellent work.

It makes me think of a salesperson who travels each week for their company. One could see that as the salesperson doing their job, but imagine what would happen if at the next staff meeting someone gave a shout-out to this person and said:

There are two things you do a lot of: traveling and selling. But there's a lot people don't know about. Things like the 3:30 a.m. alarm for your early flight the other day that accidentally woke up your newborn. Or that time a few weeks ago when your flight home was delayed, which caused you to miss your wife's birthday dinner. And the reason no one knows about these two instances is because you don't make a big deal out of them. You have a way of taking these things in stride. But we see you and know this job can take a toll on all aspects of your life. We also know that our customers love you. Being excellent at your job and caring for our customers so well makes all of us better and allows this company to thrive. Thank you for all you do!

How long would that take in a meeting? Maybe thirty seconds? But think of how it'd make that salesperson feel.

When we recognize others and make them feel valued, we end up feeling valued too. We're all breathing that same air.

I enjoyed this experience at EntreLeadership so much that I immediately incorporated shout-outs into our staff meetings. They became one of my favorite parts of the week. And the day we get too busy to pause for a little recognition is the day I'll say we've lost the plot.

You don't have to be the person calling a meeting to instigate shout-outs. In fact, there doesn't even need to be an official shout-out time for this to be incorporated into your work culture. You don't need anyone's permission. You can take different opportunities to let people know the impact their work is making, whether or not you're in front of others. And you may be surprised at how quickly others respond in a similar way.

Encouraging words are like currency. There's value in telling others how much you appreciate them. Give away recognition like a philanthropist gives away money.

Keep in mind it doesn't have to be a public display of appreciation either. Not everyone enjoys public recognition. But just because someone doesn't enjoy the limelight doesn't mean they don't want to feel appreciated. It can be as simple as leaving a handwritten note on their desk. Written acknowledgment can be just as powerful as verbal acknowledgment.

Indra Nooyi, former chairman and CEO of PepsiCo, did this in a unique way. She wrote notes of appreciation to her employees'

GIVE AWAY
RECOGNITION
— LIKE A —
PHILANTHROPIST
GIVES AWAY
MONEY.

TIM SCHURRER

parents. Indra was inspired during a trip to India to visit her mother, when she saw visitor after visitor congratulate her mother on raising a daughter who became CEO of such a successful company. It got her thinking: "We owe so much of our success to our parents, and they never get credit for the role they play in their children's lives."[3] Soon after she got back from her trip, she started writing thank-you notes to her employees' parents, congratulating them on raising their children and thanking them for what an asset their family has been for PepsiCo. Unsurprisingly, both the parents and the employees were deeply moved by this expression of gratitude.

Can you imagine the impact this has on both families and company culture?

Our team at StoryBrand adopted this culture of recognition, and none more than the CEO, Donald Miller. We made a big deal out of people's work anniversaries. It was important to us to celebrate the years people invested in the company and the contributions they made day after day.

This isn't the case at all companies, though.

It was my friend Travis's work anniversary; he had been with his company for ten years. Wondering what his team would do to celebrate him, he drove to the office with an extra dose of excitement. There was nothing on his desk when he got there, but he kept thinking that at any moment his coworkers would surprise him with something big. Hour by hour his excitement faded, and he began to wonder if anyone had even remembered. 2:00 p.m. . . . 3:00 p.m. . . . 4:00 p.m. . . . nothing. Finally, at 5:00 p.m., Travis accepted his fate. Everyone had forgotten. Ten years and not a single person had stopped to recognize him with even a simple congratulations.

My friend Bob says we can choose to be *reflections of or*

reactions to the people and things we experience. What happened to Travis was something we never wanted to happen at our company. In fact, for my five-year work anniversary, Don surprised me with a really nice gift. He came into my office that day and handed me a wrapped box. I opened it to find a beautiful watch. But it was the handwritten note, along with the watch, that brought me to tears:

> What you have accomplished in the last five years has been stunning. You have built a company, but more than a company, you have built a community. At StoryBrand, people love each other because of the tone you have set and the person that you are. It is a very hard thing to build a company. Only a small percentage of those who try, succeed. But you didn't just make it, you built a company that thrives. It is growing, and we are all growing with it. You make things better when you walk in the room. We are who we are, a loving, competent community because of you.
>
> I got you a gift to always remind you of this milestone. But it's really not for you. It's for your son. If, in the distant future, he ever has a challenge, you can give it to him and remind him that it is in him to do a hard thing well.
>
> Love,
> Don

Can you imagine the energy I felt from being celebrated like that? Words have power, especially when they're delivered from someone you respect. Leaders taking the time to write a few sentences of encouragement can create lift for weeks, if not for months or years.

We made an effort to recognize the value Don brought to the

team as well. Remember: leaders need to feel seen and appreciated just like anyone else.

I got this text from a team member a few years ago, after we had been in a video shoot with Don earlier in the day:

> The way Don communicates is so precise. I learn a freaking ton about communicating clearly from him, especially when we are in these video shoots. It's easy to get bogged down in the details of production and logistics, but it's so huge that we get to learn like this. He's so good. It pisses me off ;)

I then sent a note to Don "It's important you know what people say about you behind your back :)" and included a screenshot of my team member's text.

It's a privilege to be part of a team that is committed to recognizing its people. But it's not the only way that you, as a Secret Society member, can experience the power of feeling noticed.

AND IF THEY DON'T FOLLOW MY LEAD?

What do you do when you're faced with a work culture that just doesn't appreciate you? What if, no matter what you do, it seems like no one wants to take even baby steps in that direction?

Well, you have a choice to make.

You can play the victim and feel bad about yourself. You can believe the lie that this will never get better for you, that this is just the hand you've been dealt. You can fall into the trap of the Spotlight Mindset and start demanding attention and recognition, perhaps even at the expense of your relationships. You can quit your job and find something else. You can believe a better team is out there, waiting for you to be a part of it. You can go from job to job, looking for a company with a healthy culture of recognition. You can waste time, energy, and money, making pivot after pivot. But finding this kind of work culture is not a guarantee.

Any of those options would be fair in light of the circumstances. However, you don't necessarily have to give up, quit, or change jobs to feel appreciated.

I want to present an alternative to you. One that will provide you with much more satisfaction and joy in your life. One that initiates you into the Secret Society. The solution is to turn inward and find an internal drive, the motivation to keep going simply by doing the work. When you do this, you'll find that, ironically, the external circumstances will inevitably begin to shift. But even without that guarantee, you'll find that the work itself is the reward. (We'll talk about this at length in chapter 8.)

Sound impossible? I'd argue that a differentiating quality of those in the Secret Society is their internal drive. They are able to reach down and find the motivation to do their work, not for the praise or attention, but for the work itself and for the good they know it accomplishes.

VALUE DOESN'T EQUAL RECOGNITION

One of our biggest problems isn't that we want to be seen and valued (that's just being human); it's that we tie certain kinds of recognition so closely to our value and depend on them to affirm that value. In Chris Hedges's book *Empire of Illusion*, he explained:

Celebrity and connectivity are both ways of becoming known. This is what the contemporary self wants. It wants to be recognized, wants to be connected: It wants to be visible. If not to the millions, on *Survivor* or *Oprah*, then to the hundreds, on Twitter or Facebook. This is the quality that validates us, this is how we become real to ourselves—by being seen by others. The great contemporary terror is anonymity.[4]

Why are we so scared of anonymity? It's because we've linked our value to recognition. We've linked our worth to getting noticed. But our value does not have to come from being on a stage, being seen, or being recognized.

It's not that simple to divorce recognition with value. When you're not getting recognition, it's easy to get in your head, distracted by the thought that you're not worthwhile. Rather than allow these thoughts to pull you into a negative spiral, consider how you might turn the ship around by becoming a person who actively spreads recognition.

You might think, *Well, that solves the problem for other people, but not for me! I can't make people recognize my work.* It's true that you can't control other people, but you can contribute to an environment that promotes the recognition of others for the work they do. That environment will eventually feed you too.

If we truly want to change the culture in businesses all over the world, we need to band together as a Secret Society and make recognition a part of our daily routines.

My dream is that one day our workplaces will be filled with more people—the CEO and every other position at a company—with their heads on a swivel, keeping an eye out for the work others are doing that might go unnoticed. That one day, bosses will see the work their teams are doing behind the scenes and let them know they appreciate them. That one day, team members will take the time to recognize and appreciate their bosses. And, that one day, teams all over the country will add shout-outs to their staff meetings, creating a support system that makes people feel seen and cared for.

We can only control what we can control, and I'd like to echo the advice to "be the change that you wish to see in the world." Be a person who regularly gives recognition to others, whether or not you ever receive it in return.

I hope you choose to become an advocate for your colleagues. As a member of the Secret Society, you make it a point to call people out for the amazing work no one else notices and, ultimately, make others feel valued and a little less invisible.

Even more, I hope you learn that your value isn't tied to how much you are recognized. Instead of spending time raising your hand for attention, spend it on building something you're passionate about. It doesn't have to be grand. In fact, whatever it is, I bet it starts small.

The
WAY TO DO
REALLY BIG
THINGS
SEEMS TO BE
TO START WITH
DECEPTIVELY SMALL
THINGS.

PAUL GRAHAM

6

YOU DON'T
NEED A STAGE

When we hear about successful companies, it's easy to forget their humble beginnings—when the team was only a handful of people, if even that many. As we set our sights to emulate the success we see, we often aim for a company or a role that is several steps ahead of where we are today, and then we get frustrated that it's taking so long to get what we want. We want to have the type of impact we see others have, but without having to experience the building phases. We want immediate success.

This is true not only for entrepreneurs but also for those who are part of larger teams and companies. The fancy office on the top floor has a certain appeal to it. To have the power to delegate whatever we don't want to do and have people assist *us* would be nice. We dream of skipping steps and not having to deal with the current day-to-day.

The corner office, the millions of products sold, the big

company, and the big reach are examples of platforms or stages. Having a big platform or standing on a stage is not a bad thing. It can be a great opportunity to do a lot of good. The misconception here, however, is that a stage will be what makes us happy, that it will be the thing that validates all the sacrifices we've made or the key to unlocking satisfaction in our lives. This is a lie of the Spotlight Mindset.

The Spotlight Mindset says you need a stage to:

- launch a business or idea
- be significant
- impress people
- have a successful career

But the Secret Society doesn't care so much about stages. Instead, those in the Secret Society focus on one impacted life at a time. And you'd be surprised where that can lead a person.

If you're constantly playing a *soundtrack*, as my friend Jon Acuff calls it, in your head that says "I need a platform, a stage," "What I have isn't enough," "I need to do more," "My life only counts if I touch thousands or millions of people," you'll find yourself perpetually unhappy and exhausted.

You do have another option, though.

You can, as Jon recommends in his book *Soundtracks*, replace a broken soundtrack with a new one.[1] You could tell yourself something like this instead: "One life at a time. Let that be enough."

At the risk of spoiling the ending, that's what this chapter is all about. This mentality has been adopted by those in the Secret Society, and it is one you can adopt too.

Perhaps the "one life at a time" approach will compound over years and years, and one day you'll find yourself running a large company or a team. Think of the solid foundation you'll be operating from. You'll be less concerned about the size of your reach and more focused on the depth of your interactions with each individual. But we'll get to this.

First, let me tell you about a Secret Society member Blake Mycoskie. This is the story about how his company, TOMS, grew from a simple idea to the fastest-growing shoe brand in the world.

How? One life at a time.

LAUNCHING A GLOBAL SHOE BRAND

Blake wasn't even trying to start a global shoe brand. As a serial entrepreneur, he had started several different businesses by the time he was in his midtwenties. In the midst of running one of these companies, he needed a break and traveled to Argentina to learn to play polo.

A few weeks into the trip, he was in a wine bar when he heard a couple of English-speaking women. When he approached them and asked what they were doing in Argentina, he learned they were there to give away shoes. These women gathered gently used shoes from wealthy families in Buenos Aires and gave them to kids in the surrounding less-fortunate villages. Since shoes were a part of the school uniform, kids weren't allowed to go to school without them. A lot of families in these villages didn't own a pair of shoes for every child, so they would rotate who had the shoes, and, therefore, who could go to school.

The women asked Blake if he was interested in joining them for one of their giving adventures, and he did the very next week.

Little did Blake know he was about to experience something that would change his life forever.

That night Blake debriefed the whole experience with his polo teacher, Alejo. He shared everything from the challenges these families were up against to the simple solution shoes offered. Alejo then asked Blake a haunting question: "What happens when the kids wear out those shoes or grow out of them?"

Blake had an idea. What if he could sell a pair of shoes to someone in the United States and have that purchase fund the gift of a pair of shoes to someone in need? It was a simple but revolutionary concept. Keep in mind this idea wasn't created to disrupt the business landscape. Blake was simply trying to sell shoes to people at home with the hope that by the following Christmas he could bring back 250 pairs to Argentina, one for each child in the village he had visited.

Alpargatas are the everyday shoe of Argentina, but they're a unique style to Americans, a style Blake had a hunch would sell. He worked with Argentinian shoemakers to create some prototypes, and soon boarded a flight to Los Angeles with 250 pairs. Blake now had a side project, what he called a "personal, fun philanthropic experiment."[2]

In Los Angeles, he sold the alpargatas to everyone he could, and even had the retailer American Rag agree to sell them in their store. The leading fashion writer for the *Los Angeles Times* caught wind of the story of the shoes and interviewed Blake. The day after the article ran in the paper, they had 2,200 orders.

No typo there. Twenty. Two. Hundred. Quite a few more than the 250 he'd brought over.

This was a massive problem.

Blake flew back to Argentina and immediately headed to one of the shoemakers he'd worked with on the prototypes, and said three very important words: *"Muchos zapatos rápido!"* (Many shoes fast!).

It took several weeks to fulfill that first wave of orders, and Blake was recruiting help like crazy to keep customer service under control. The business was off like a rocket and has hardly looked back since.

The first shoe drop (what TOMS calls their giving trips) exceeded expectations. They distributed not only the 250 pairs they had hoped for but an additional 10,000 to the Argentinian children.

While the *Los Angeles Times* article helped get TOMS on the map, it was a *Vogue* feature not too long after, that blew the roof off. The company did $300,000 in revenue the first year, $3 million the second, $15 million the third, $60 million the fourth, and within seven years they were at $450 million. "We became the fastest-growing shoe company in the world," Blake explained. "It was insane."[3]

The revolutionary business model of "one for one" was making an impact one child and one village at a time.

By whatever scoreboard you look at, Blake has been successful. But he didn't get there by vying for the spotlight, and he certainly didn't write "(1) sell 95 million pairs of shoes, and (2) disrupt the fashion industry with a revolutionary business model by giving away half of your product" on any kind of goals worksheet.

These two things did happen, though. And it started without a platform. Blake was moved to help kids in a single village get shoes so they could go to school, and he dove in headfirst, without regard for where it would all lead.

HELPING WOMEN COME OFF THE
STREETS IN NASHVILLE

Becca Stevens had a challenging childhood. When she was five years old, her father was killed by a drunk driver. Not too long after that she was a victim of sexual abuse by a family friend. But what's remarkable about Becca was her response to this trauma.

In 1997, Becca, then in her midthirties, had befriended several women who were living on the streets, and she wanted to help them so they, too, could heal from the wounds they were suffering from. Becca raised the funds and opened the doors of a house in Nashville to five women, and those women began their healing journey, no longer having to live on the streets to survive.

A few years into this, the recovery component was going really well, but the women were struggling to become financially self-sufficient because getting a normal job was difficult for them. Imagine having a criminal record and trying to get a job in today's market. It's nearly impossible. So Becca, along with the residents of this house and some volunteers, began making candles in a church basement to sell and provide income. In 2001, they officially launched this business and called it Thistle Farms.

Whenever someone meets a prostitute or a homeless person on the streets, a common question is "What'd you do?" And with that question comes the judgment, "You must have done something to deserve this life you're living." This is a dangerous perspective. I've learned from Becca, "None of the women we serve at Thistle Farms ended up on the streets by themselves. It took a whole bunch of broken systems and broken communities who really rolled out the red carpet. That story is borne by the women of Thistle Farms, who on average are first raped between the ages of seven and eleven, and first hit the streets between the ages of fourteen and sixteen."[4]

"Women don't just choose to be on the streets or selling themselves," said Regina, who has been through recovery and is now the outreach coordinator at Thistle Farms. "If you go back, you will find some traumatic circumstances that have happened in each woman's life that have made them feel like 'this is all I have' or 'this is the only way that I'm going to get someone to love me.'"[5]

The approach at Thistle Farms is unique. They don't ask, "What did you do?" They ask, "What happened to you?" This approach allows these women to heal from their trauma. Becca has a foundational belief that women deserve a second chance at life. She said, "But the amazing thing to me is, for many of the women we serve, this is their *first* chance at life. They entered into trafficking at the age of five or six, they never had a fair shake. And this may be the first time a community has invested in them to say 'now's your time.'"[6]

What started with a single house of five women in 1997 has grown to multiple houses over the years. There are now six hundred long-term, free beds available for women survivors across the country in the Thistle Farms network. Not only this, they have more than thirty global partnerships and have helped launch another five justice enterprises. Thousands of women have experienced recovery from abuse, drug addiction, and prostitution.

Thistle Farms is based in Nashville, and on Wednesday mornings, in their production facility off Charlotte Avenue and Fifty-First Street, they welcome the public to join their morning meditation. Regardless of whether there are ten people or fifty, everyone circles up, and, in the center of the room, they light a candle. Then everyone says in unison, "We light the candle for the woman still out there, suffering and searching for a way home. We light the candle for the baby born into addiction without a choice in the matter. We light the candle for the woman who needs to cut a path through the darkest night."

I have joined the group for several Wednesday meditations, and every time I go, I am grateful I did. You gain so much perspective on what truly matters in a short amount of time. Meeting women with the courage to get off the streets and engage in the hard work of recovery is inspiring.

First-timers are invited to tour the production facility after the meditation is over. One of the women in the program or recently graduated from the program leads the tour, showing newcomers how they make the Thistle Farms products.

Jennifer often leads these tours, and throughout the walk around the facility, she shares her story and tells people about the recovery she experienced as a result of Thistle Farms. There was a season when I had a new person with me often, and so I'd join them on this first-timer tour. I became fast friends with Jennifer, my favorite tour guide.

By hearing stories from Jennifer, I began to understand the depth of the impact Thistle Farms was making on this community of women.

HITTING ROCK BOTTOM

Before meeting Becca, Jennifer lived in her car on the streets of Dayton, Ohio. One night she was getting dangerously low on gas and was afraid the fuel line might freeze from the subzero temperatures. Without intermittent starts, the temperature inside her car would soon match the temperature outside. Even though she was homeless, Jennifer avoided the overnight shelters. But with a growing concern she may run out of gas by the evening, she didn't have much of a choice.

It had been so long since her last visit to the shelter that she couldn't remember where it was and decided to ask someone for help. While stopped at the next traffic light, she rolled down the passenger window and got the attention of a young woman in the car next to her.

"Hey there. Uhh. Do you know how to get to the homeless shelter from here? I'm a bit lost," she said.

The response she received, however, was nothing like she expected. "Mom! Don't you recognize me?"

Jennifer's heart sank. She hadn't recognized her own daughter. Not only that, because of the life she had been living on the streets, she didn't even realize her daughter was now old enough to drive.

As she wrote in her memoir, "One hellish day after another had turned into sixteen years. Total oblivion."[7]

For several decades, Jennifer survived life on the streets as a prostitute. To give you an idea of the living hell she experienced: she was sexually and physically abused as a child, she began living on her own at age thirteen, she gave birth to two children who died, several of her friends were either murdered or died from drug overdoses, and she was the victim of numerous rapes and beatings. The list actually goes on and on.

Just one of those traumatic events would be enough to throw anyone into a severe depression or possibly drive them to suicide. How Jennifer experienced all of that and survived is a miracle in and of itself. But without an intervention, that might not have been the case.

"My main daily goal was to get so polluted that I was basically unconscious. I wanted it like that. I didn't want to remember any-thing," Jennifer wrote. "I started working in the sex industry in the so-called Gentlemen's Clubs. Every time I sold myself and used drugs, another piece of me died. It ended with an over-eighteen-year IV heroin addiction. Streetwalking. Homelessness. Jails. Psych wards. Rehabs. My life had evolved into an inten-tional unconsciousness."[8]

One night, a man she trusted pushed her head through a glass window. This was her breaking point. She had had enough.

"I want to come home," she told her sister from the nearest pay phone.

She must have heard the desperation in Jennifer's voice, because her sister simply said, "Okay."

Her sister's response was a bit surprising. The only time Jennifer called her family was if she needed money, so they avoided her as a way of showing their disapproval of her lifestyle. That lack of support was part of a vicious cycle that kept her on the streets. Unaddressed trauma, living in a community of people who were making bad decisions, little outside support, and no real purpose for living is a dangerous recipe.

Jennifer tried to kill herself many times, but, by the grace of God, she survived every attempt. That alone caused her to believe there must be a reason she was still alive. Surely she had some purpose. Some community of people to serve.

After moving in with her sister and getting her feet under her, Jennifer decided she wanted to talk to a priest and ask for her sins to be forgiven. While her sister waited in the car, she spent almost two hours with the priest and immediately felt a weight being lifted from her. When she got back, her sister said it was the first time she had seen a genuine smile from her in years.

Before leaving the priest, Jennifer asked him for help. Surely there had to be a place she could go to recover from all she'd experienced. He told her he'd look into it. The next day she received a call from the priest, who told her about a place in Nashville she could go. There was a two-year program with an opening where she could get the help she needed.

Jennifer was skeptical. She had been to places like this before. Eventually the recovery centers would charge rent from the people in the program, and it would tip the domino that would put her back on the streets, since the only way she knew to make money was by doing the thing she was trying to recover from. And when you step back into that lifestyle, you end up staying there, because it is familiar.

"Jen, this is a free program. No rent. Nothing," the priest told her.

She couldn't believe her ears. Maybe this time it would truly be different, she thought.

That night was several years ago. Jennifer no longer lives on the streets of Dayton and has made a 180-degree turn from the life she lived for so many years. Addiction and prostitution are just past memories. That's not who she is anymore. Thanks in large part to Becca Stevens.

While the intention was never to start a global movement, that's exactly what's happened with Thistle Farms.

"After a couple years of meeting with survivors and witnessing miracles of healing love, I knew I would be doing this work for the rest of my life," Becca wrote in her book *Love Heals*. "The survivor-leaders were living with a new power and grace that I knew could potentially bring healing throughout the entire world."[9]

It's easy to find Becca onstage, jumping from city to city, spreading the word about Thistle Farms. In fact, if you saw her calendar, you'd wonder how she gets it all done without being completely exhausted every day. But while it's a lot to manage, the stories of the lives she's changing keep her going.

When I asked Jennifer where she'd be without Becca Stevens's influence in her life, she responded without hesitation, "I'd be dead. Without Becca, I'd be dead."

Becca has been fortunate. She's been at this for a long time now and gets to see up close the impact she's made. But even if all this work had gotten just one life off the streets, someone like Jennifer, it would have been worth it. One life at a time.

Perhaps you've been doing your work for a long time, and you aren't seeing the type of impact you dreamed of. Or maybe you're waiting to move on your big idea until you build a bigger platform. What if you shifted your focus to just "one life"? Would that be enough for you to feel content?

We are bombarded by this idea that to actually have a meaningful life we have to have some kind of stage or platform. We have to be a world changer. But does world changer have to mean thousands or millions of people? Becca Stevens changed Jennifer's entire world.

My hope is that by approaching life in the way of the Secret Society, you'll turn down that outside voice telling you you're not successful unless you have a bigger reach. You don't need a stage to make an impact.

One life at a time. Let that be enough.

RELATIONALLY WEALTHY

I was in the car listening to a podcast when I heard Drew Holcomb casually mention the topic of his college dissertation. He was

YOU DON'T NEED — A — STAGE TO MAKE AN IMPACT.

TIM SCHURRER

@TIMSCHURRER / SECRETSOCIETYBOOK.COM

sharing a bit about his childhood and about growing up with a brother with special needs. He said, referring to his brother, "My college dissertation was about the impact of a single person's life on a community."[10] I'd known Drew for years, but I didn't know much about his family. I tracked down a copy of his dissertation, and then called Drew to learn more.

His brother, Jay, had been born with spina bifida, which is when a baby's spinal cord doesn't properly develop and can cause varying levels of disability. For some, it limits how they move and function and could land them in a wheelchair for the entirety of their lives. It's rare to see those diagnosed with spina bifida live into their thirties, with many passing away at much younger ages. Unfortunately, this was the case for Jay, who lived a remarkable thirteen years. Thousands of people attended his funeral to honor his life. Why were so many people compelled to show up?

Jay didn't spend his energy on the scoreboards the world tells us to pay attention to. Instead, with phone calls, questions, smiles, and thousands of small kindnesses, he deposited coin after coin into relationships.

At the funeral, their dad delivered the eulogy. "Jay had no job, $400 to his name, never played on a sports team, never had a girlfriend, had a gnarly looking body, and yet," he said, and then gestured to the audience, "despite Jay's failures at what the world deems success, he had gone out triumphantly being celebrated and mourned by many."[11] He concluded, very simply, "Jay died relationally wealthy."

Jay had no platform of any kind. He passed away three days before his fourteenth birthday. And yet he found a way to impact an entire community. No stage necessary.

WHERE TO START: RIGHT WHERE YOU ARE

The Spotlight Mindset steals our focus away from people and puts it on our position. And when we're focused on position and the validation we get from that position, we'll never be satisfied. When we buy into the Spotlight Mindset, we exhaust ourselves trying to make it to the next level, to a bigger stage, or we make excuses for not even starting: "When I'm manager, then I'll make a change around here." "When I have x number of followers, then I'll start sharing about my passions." "When I finally make it, then I'll be able to have an impact."

In my opinion, aiming for a big stage misses the point: any impact on any life matters, and that's where you can start. You don't need to wait until you have the perfect job or are higher up on the ladder. You can start looking for ways to make a difference now. And I think you'll be amazed at the positive ripple effect this will have on your life.

What is most impactful to me about Blake's and Becca's stories is that while they are now operating from a place of influence, they didn't get there by trying to get there. Their approach has been to focus on individuals, and over the years those individuals have accumulated a pretty significant impact on millions of lives. I also think of Jay, and the people he touched with the same approach.

No matter our trajectory, the Secret Society encourages us to start small, to measure ourselves not by where we're standing but by those we're impacting. One life at a time.

LIFE'S MOST PERSISTENT AND URGENT QUESTION IS, "WHAT ARE YOU DOING FOR OTHERS?"

MARTIN LUTHER KING JR.

LET A
PROBLEM BE YOUR
SOLUTION

Who would have thought a guy wearing zip-up sweaters and sing-ing children's songs would become a national icon? More popularly known as Mister Rogers, Fred starred in the children's television show *Mister Rogers' Neighborhood.* When he talked about difficult issues such as divorce and death, Fred reassured his young audience and taught them how to navigate their childhood. He had a way onscreen that was disarming, kind, deep, and accessible. His message was simple: love your neighbor.

After he passed, several films have tried to bottle up his magic. *Won't You Be My Neighbor* came out in 2018, and I saw it with a group of friends. What struck me about that film—and about Fred's life—was he didn't set out to be a television star. He simply saw a need for quality television programming for children and filled that need.

At the start of Fred's career, television was relatively new. He watched the popular content being fed to children, and while it was mindless and entertaining, it wasn't helpful or educational. This troubled him, and he started an adventure to be a part of the solution, even though he had no formal training in television production.

The career path for Fred Rogers wasn't linear. He majored in music composition in college and was planning to study theology after that, but then this new passion for television emerged. While working a handful of supporting roles on various television programs, he attended seminary and then earned a degree in child psychology.

> I'll never forget the sense of wholeness I felt when I finally realized . . . I was not just a songwriter or a language buff or a student of human development or a telecommunicator, but someone who could use every talent that had ever been given to me in the service of children and their families.[1]

He chased the answer to the question "What problem can I solve?" and was gaining some traction. Fifteen years into his television journey, Fred was given the opportunity to host what we know today as *Mister Rogers' Neighborhood*.

As we look to the Secret Society to show us a way forward, it's people like Fred Rogers who illuminate the next step: look for a problem to solve.

MY SHOT

The Spotlight Mindset has us asking a different question, though. Remember WIIFM? (What's in it for me?) It's a trap, and it will do everything it can to suck you in. This is why we regularly need the influence of the Secret Society in our lives. In moments we're pulled into WIIFM thinking, we can pivot 180 degrees and ask, "What problem can I solve for someone else?" This question has a completely different focus, and it will lead to a completely different outcome.

There have been times I've given WIIFM too much of my attention. Let me share a particularly poignant example.

As I've told you, when I was an aspiring musician, John Mayer was who I wanted to be. The problem was, he was on a completely different level. He was selling out arenas, winning Grammys, and his records were going platinum. Me? I was struggling to get booked at venues, and the records I ordered with my songs on them were mostly unsold and in boxes in my garage. I couldn't wrap my mind around the idea of being John Mayer. There were just too many steps for me to take to get to where he was.

But there were others I admired and wanted to be like. I started paying attention to a talented singer-songwriter named Matt Wertz. And while he was not selling out arenas, he'd sold thousands and thousands of records, was touring nationally, and had a rapidly growing fan base. All as an independent artist, which was remarkable.

I tried learning everything about his business that I could. I'd read the liner notes of his CDs to find out the names of the musicians who played on his records. I'd study his website to see the venues he was playing in and pay careful attention to how he routed his tours. I'd be at every show of his within one hundred miles of Kansas City, often volunteering to sell his merchandise to learn that part of the business as well. I was trying to reverse engineer his success to my level and then follow his path to a T.

Whatever Matt was doing seemed to work for him. News of him seemed to spread rapidly, naturally. I knew this from personal experience. Some of my friends came back from camp at a place called Young Life, where Matt was the musical guest for the week. They bought his CDs, and he quickly became "everyone at camp's favorite artist" (their words).

If you haven't heard of Young Life, it's an organization that invests in the lives of high school students. While there's a faith affiliation, the goal of the student leaders—often young adults or college-aged students—is simply to show up in kids' lives. That could look like cheering them on at their sporting events, being there at the end of the school day to say hello, or even grabbing a cup of coffee and talking about life and faith.

Every summer, leaders invite kids to camp. There are Young Life camps all over the country, often in beautiful settings. One of the coolest camps I've ever seen is a couple of hours outside of Vancouver, British Columbia, fifty miles from the nearest road. It sits at the foot of a mountain, surrounded by water and pine trees that seem to touch the base of the clouds.

These high school students experience a week of adventure, fun, and even hear from some guest speakers and musicians. It's pretty common for the camp musicians to do a residency for a month at a time, with a new group of students cycling through every week.

My ears perked up when I learned about life as a camp musician. "So you're telling me that Matt was able to play in front of hundreds of high school kids at a time?" I asked my friend who'd just returned from camp. "With buses of soon-to-be fans arriving each week for an entire month? And everyone was buying his CDs?"

I was wide-eyed at the thought of gaining a bunch of new

fans, particularly fans who might go back to their hometown and get people excited about my music. Visualizing the boxes of CDs stacked in my garage, I knew I had to find a way to play at a Young Life camp. This would solve my problem.

I'd heard that Young Life liked to give these opportunities to "their own," meaning a majority of the camp musicians were people who were involved in the organization year-round, not just over the summer. So I had the perfect solution. I would become a student leader. I volunteered, built relationships with high school students, and kept my name front and center with Young Life in hope that I would get an invite to play at a summer camp.

You can imagine how ecstatic I was when I received an invitation.

With how effective the camps were in building a fan base for Matt, I started to believe this would be the path to my big break. Young Life would be the way I'd finally be discovered.

While a lot of these summer assignments (as they're called by Young Life insiders) were four weeks long, mine was only for one. It was a short session at the tail end of the summer for junior high students. But, hey, one week was better than no weeks. "I was young, scrappy and hungry," and "I was not throwin' away my shot," or at least that's how it felt to me.[2] This was my moment.

I was up against a welcome challenge: How will I take advantage of this opportunity to get me closer to where I want to go?

All I needed to do was execute the plan Matt had set before me, though he didn't know he'd given me a plan. I had confidence in the plan because it'd worked for him, and at the same time it supported a great organization.

But if I'm honest, I wasn't there for the kids. I wasn't asking if there was a problem I could solve for someone else. I was there for myself.

That's where all of this went wrong.

HOW WE'RE TEMPTED TO
MANIPULATE RELATIONSHIPS

Have you ever had a friend in an MLM (a multilevel marketing company)? Or perhaps you've been part of one yourself. The way an MLM works is that reps sign up to sell a product; not only that, they recruit other salespeople under them and get a commission from their team's sales as well as their own. The more you and your team sell, the higher your status. And often these top-selling reps will be incentivized with cars and financial bonuses to maintain their status, which is fueled by product sales and recruiting more reps.

The appeal to get involved in an MLM is strong. To control your own schedule and be in charge of your own income seems like a dream side hustle. And, over time, the side hustle could even become the main gig. Many people end up making a really nice income through MLMs, and many believe wholeheartedly in the products they sell.

But despite the benefits, I don't think MLMs set you up to live in the way of the Secret Society. While most reps believe they're solving a problem for their customers, I think the business model sets them up to focus first on their own success.

Perhaps you've been there. You are with a friend who's part of an MLM, and say, you're at a restaurant. Your friend starts chatting up the server. It seems harmless enough, but you have seen this before and know what's behind it. Unfortunately, you know your friend is not actually this interested in the server's life. What's happening is that she wants the server to sign up under her in the MLM. She wants to rise to the next level. She wants to get the status, the benefits. She's trying to hit her monthly numbers. Out of politeness you sit through the meal while she builds a rapport with the server until the check arrives. This is the moment your friend makes her pitch and asks the server to join her team.

The whole thing feels gross, doesn't it?

This is not exclusive to MLMs. Many salespeople can come across this way. It's not that sales, or MLMs for that matter, cannot be done well. It's that using people and relationships for the sole purpose of getting ahead in *your* job just doesn't feel right. At least for those in the Secret Society.

But let's not throw just MLMs and salespeople under the bus. We all do this. Isn't this what I was doing with those students at the Young Life camp? We use other people to solve our problems, to hit our numbers, to make it. What's worse, this is culturally acceptable. This is what we've been taught to do.

We've been hijacked by the Spotlight Mindset. When I have enough emotional distance to look at my own life and see that, I can say, "No thanks. If that's success, I don't want it."

Fortunately, there's another way.

Instead of looking for people to solve *our* problems (WIIFM), what if we started looking for ways to solve other people's problems? And I don't mean "I have a product that'll solve your problem," and then have it be a Trojan horse to your own benefit. That's not what I'm talking about. I mean the "no strings attached" approach. Helping people solve their problems. Period.

NOTHING ON THE OTHER SIDE OF THE EQUAL SIGN

Two years into running a private counseling practice in Nashville, Al Andrews noticed a unique trend. Of the people who walked

INSTEAD OF LOOKING
FOR PEOPLE TO SOLVE
OUR PROBLEMS,
— *what if* —
WE STARTED LOOKING
FOR **WAYS** TO SOLVE
OTHER PEOPLE'S
PROBLEMS?

TIM SCHURRER

through his door, most of them were in the music business. Specifically, they were artists, people whose faces were on the covers of albums. He also noticed, because of their touring schedules, they weren't able to come as frequently as his other clients. Not only this, but especially for those early in their career, they struggled to afford regular counseling sessions.

A friend suggested Al meet with Peter York, who was running a major record label in Nashville. As the president of that label, Peter was ultimately responsible for the success of dozens of artists' careers. At that meeting, Al explained the unique challenges these musicians faced. "They don't know how to navigate the career they're chasing, and it has the potential to completely ruin them if left unattended," he said. "Record labels invest hundreds of thousands, if not millions of dollars, into making these artists successful, but not a dollar is spent caring for their souls."

Little did Al know that Peter and his company had been having this same discussion recently. In fact, Peter had been charged with finding a way to help their artists, so when Al came to him with this, it was further confirmation they were on to something important.

Not long after their conversation, the two men outlined a pilot project. For the next three months Al would block one day a week for artists to book counseling sessions at no charge. The fees would be paid by the record label with one stipulation: Al would have to be willing to see artists from any label, not just those Peter was responsible for.

The sessions that followed during the three-month pilot period were a huge success. Artists found a place they could go offstage to talk with someone in confidence about everything that was challenging them. But not only that, they found a guide, someone who would walk with them on their journey toward health.

After the pilot program, Al and Peter met again—this time to figure out how to keep this program going long-term. In the end, Al converted his private practice into a 501(c)(3) nonprofit organization and made the decision to focus his counseling work exclusively on helping recording artists.

What started with Al being booked one day a week with artists became five days a week, and it was Peter's company and other record labels that covered the bill. Al named the organization Porter's Call, which was fitting given that porters at Benedictine monasteries welcomed the sojourners and helped them find their way to what they needed, whether that be food, a place to stay, or wise counsel.

Since 2001, Porter's Call has grown to a staff of five and has helped thousands of artists navigate their world in the spotlight. While this work—as is true with all counseling practices—is done in confidence, several artists have spoken out as advocates so that fellow artists can take advantage of the opportunity to get help:

> They always tell you that all your dreams are gonna come true, but they don't tell you at what cost. I think the smartest thing labels and management teams could invest in is the mental and emotional well-being of their signed artists. To not consider the human element at the core of the music industry is to literally risk tragic fate again and again without seeing the cause. Porter's Call has been a huge help to me, my bandmates, and many of my friends in this industry. I'm forever grateful.
>
> —HAYLEY WILLIAMS OF PARAMORE

Porter's Call has taught me how to stay true to myself and to use fame as a platform to do good in this world rather than a place to boost my ego, lose sense of who I am, or wreck my marriage. Being on the road can be challenging, especially for a married artist, but my wife and I have been truly encouraged by Porter's Call. They do not sugarcoat the truth, which in turn leaves us feeling confident knowing the truth about the challenges we have faced and soon will face—and how to successfully manage those situations.

—THOMAS RHETT

We lost my grandfather and countless other musicians who couldn't find a sturdy place to land. Because of Porter's Call, lives are changing, marriages are rising from the ashes, children are experiencing a more stable home, addictions are being broken, and, most importantly, the artists and musicians are able to soar.

**—HOLLY WILLIAMS, ARTIST AND
GRANDDAUGHTER OF HANK WILLIAMS**[3]

Porter's Call has been a massive success because of the posture they've taken in running their organization. From the very start, they have been focused around "What problem can I solve?" and have spent the past two decades caring for everyone who walks through their door. And there's no catch. No Trojan horse. Nothing on the other side of the equal sign. Simply free counseling and support to whoever needs it.

WHERE I WENT WRONG

Landing in a career you love is not an easy thing, nor is finding satisfaction in one you've been at for a while. Regardless of where you are on your career journey, the Spotlight Mindset will pull you toward WIIFM. That's where things went wrong for me when I was trying to replicate Matt Wertz's success through Young Life.

It's easy to see this now, but I wasn't in the best headspace for what I had set out to do. My plan was logical, but my motivation was too focused on my journey to the top and not on the people sitting right in front of me. I cared more about what I could get from those students at camp than what I could give them.

I wasn't intentionally being selfish. Very few of us ever are. I was operating subconsciously out of a Spotlight Mindset. I felt like I was doing what was natural and strategic, even generous. I was helping others to help myself.

The Spotlight Mindset's pull is more powerful in our lives than we'd like to admit, and it has the ability to take over our reasoning. It gets us to act out of self-interest and justifies it, whispering, "Everyone does this. It's the way of the world."

The tragedy is that this approach will slowly disconnect us from who we want to be. We may feel something is a little off, but often we lack the language to describe how we are feeling, let alone how to sort out what we are feeling. By focusing on the needs of other people, we live in integrity with the part of ourselves that wants what's best for the world.

How this particular story ended for me was that while I got my invitation to camp, not much else happened. I didn't sell many CDs, and it didn't create opportunities to play future concerts for these students or their friends back in their hometowns. It felt like I had done something wrong. *Why did this not work out for me as it had for so many other camp musicians?* The whole thing left me shaking my head, confused and discouraged.

I can't change the past, and I'm grateful for the decisions I've made, because they've brought me to where I am today.

But I often wonder what my life would have looked like had I asked a different question from the start. The students at Young Life camp came for relationships—with each other and with the staff—and to explore the big questions about faith. What if I had been more interested in fostering that experience for them rather than manipulating the situation to get me closer to my dream?

The way of the Secret Society is a better approach. Solving a problem for others is where it begins, and it's the antidote to the lack of integrity we feel when we are operating out of a WIIFM mindset.

I heard someone say, "Help enough people get what they want and eventually you'll get what you want."

The Secret Society, I'm learning, would take this a step further. For them, they would say, "Help people get what they want. Period."

So how do we get rid of the question, WIIFM?

Well, we can't simply tell ourselves not to think about ourselves. That's counterproductive. It'd be like me telling you not to think about a purple giraffe. Now all you can think about is a purple giraffe! That's a silly example, but it makes the point: you can't will yourself not to want something.

There's no off switch for our desires. There will always be this duality in you that wants to look out for yourself and that wants to help others. This is a tension you have to manage, a tension between solving your own problems and solving other people's problems.

But we *can* control our focus. We can ask ourselves new questions. What if we started asking "What problem can I solve?" a little more frequently than we do today?

That question won't erase your other motives. But it will give you something new: a problem that will require your energy and your attention. I would imagine the answers you come up with will lead you on an interesting journey, one with many demands, one that could grow into a lasting career. Like Fred Rogers, it could land you in the spotlight and impact millions. Or perhaps, like Al Andrews, your impact will be felt behind the scenes.

Both men followed their skill set, their passion, and, most importantly, what the world around them needed. The question of a problem to solve started them in the right direction. It can point us in the right direction too.

YOU MIGHT
EARN A
LIVING WITH
YOUR PURSUITS
OR YOU MIGHT NOT,
BUT YOU CAN
RECOGNIZE THAT THIS
IS *NOT REALLY*
THE POINT.

ELIZABETH GILBERT

8

GET LOST
IN THE WORK

"Hi. I'm Mike, and I'm an addict. Sixteen years ago, my daily habit was to use alcohol and drugs from the minute I woke up to the minute I passed out at night. All I wanted to do was get and stay high."[1] This was how Michael Brody-Waite opened his presentation to a roomful of business leaders.

Michael is no longer an "unemployable, homeless, thieving, lying drug addict" (his words).[2] His recovery didn't come easy, though. He participated in more than two thousand twelve-step meetings and has done the hard, uncomfortable work to experience breakthroughs while fighting his addiction, which is a daily struggle. A man once living on the streets found himself in corporate America, where he received eight promotions in eight years and led a company on the Inc. 500 list.

As a key principle in his recovery, Michael learned to surrender the outcome. "People are wasting their energy on things they can't control at the expense of things they can," he said. And, according to him, that's leading us down a dangerous path.

What would it look like to surrender the outcome and get lost in our work? What if we cared more about our work than where that work could lead us?

LEAD AND LAG MEASURES

In business, it's said that success is contingent on lead and lag measures, and so it's important to know the difference between the two. This concept was popularized by the best-selling book *The 4 Disciplines of Execution.* In it, the authors offer a helpful definition for each:

> Lag measures are the tracking measurements of the wildly important goal, and they are usually the ones you spend most of your time praying over. Revenue, profit, market share, and customer satisfaction are all lag measures, meaning that when you receive them, the performance that drove them is already in the past. That's why you're praying—by the time you get a lag measure, you can't fix it. It's history.
>
> Lead measures are quite different in that they are the measures of the most high-impact things your team must do to reach the goal. In essence, they measure the new behaviors that will drive success on the lag measures, whether those behaviors are as simple as offering a sample to every customer at the bakery or as complex as adhering to standards in a jet-engine design.
>
> A good lead measure has two basic characteristics: It's

predictive of achieving the goal and it can be influenced by the team members.[3]

Let's say you're an event business. It'd be easy to obsess over the number of registrations you have or don't have on a given day. Imagine the boss kicking off the morning staff meeting with, "Hey, team! Registrations are not what we need them to be. Today, I need you to help us get more registrations."

What's crazy is that a version of this staff meeting happens millions of times a day in companies all over the world. And that's unfortunate, because this type of message does almost no good. In this example, the team can't get more registrations (it's a lag measure). So what *can* the team do? That's why we need lead measures. Lead measures are the actions the team can take today to impact tomorrow's lag measures.

When thinking about lead measures, a more helpful staff meeting would look something like this:

Hey, team! Registrations are not what we need them to be. It's going to take all of us working together to get this back on track. I want you to think of three things you can do today that have the potential to move the needle on that registration number.

Linden, perhaps we could brainstorm an expiring offer you and the sales team could use on your outbound calls this week.

Davis, could we add a new email in the sales funnel with a powerful customer testimonial? I remember a really compelling story shared in Slack yesterday that might be a good fit.

Alicia, are there any trends we're seeing in customer service emails this week? Perhaps we could include a section on the website with answers to some of the common questions or even language that would overcome some of the resistance customers have before registering.

Do you see the difference? In this version, they talked about what they can actually control. Registrations can't be the focus. Executing the process has to be the focus, with a belief that the results will follow.

This isn't only true in the business world. Let's look at this through the lens of a NASCAR pit crew. Each member's job is to oversee one of the six roles needed in a pit stop to get their driver back on the track as fast as possible. Ideally a pit stop lasts a total of eleven or twelve seconds.[4] Their ability to execute with precision and speed is one of the contributing factors in how successful their driver and the team are in that day's race.

So it's laughable to imagine this kind of pep talk right before the race: "All right, guys. Today, let's win. Whatever we do, make sure we win."

Okay . . . thanks?

Of course winning is the goal. It is the goal for every driver and every pit crew in the race. But it does them no good to obsess about it. To set themselves up to win, each person has to own their role and become the most efficient pit crew member possible, to shave off fractions of a second from their task when replacing the tires or refueling the vehicle. That is what they're focused on. They work to improve the activity they can control (the lead measure), not to win the race (the lag measure).

This also applies to parenting. We all know parents who seemingly did everything right, but their children, one way or another, caused a lot of damage or stress. Parenting is certainly important, but there is no one-to-one correlation with how a person turns out. When it comes to being a parent, you do not have (and will never have) control over the outcome.

In fact, there are very few things in life you do have control over. You have control over your attitude, your response, and maybe even your thoughts (depending on how literal you want to be about it). But, as much as you want to pretend otherwise, you have very little control over results. So, even though you can and should control your attitude and approach in life, you have no choice but to surrender the outcome.

WHY EVEN TRY?

If we have no control over the outcome, why even try? Is it just a fool's errand to think we can influence our lives in the way we want? I believe this is exactly why it's so important we work to control our attitudes, our actions, and our responses.

Because our vision of future success can never be guaranteed, we have to be willing to do the work for the satisfaction of having done the work. Period. We must learn to be content with the journey, regardless of what happens. This is the way of the Secret Society.

How we show up and what we contribute is all we can control. Fall in love with your work—even the work of shaping your attitude—and the rest really does take care of itself.

THE SAVANNAH BANANAS

Jesse Cole is the owner of a baseball team called the Savannah Bananas. (Yes, that's really their name.) The Bananas are a minor league team based in Savannah, Georgia. How minor league? Well, ahead of them there are:

- Major leagues
- AAA
- AA
- High A
- Low A
- Short-Season A
- Advanced Rookie
- Rookie
- Professional Independent
- College

And then there's Summer Collegiate baseball, which is the league the Bananas are in. But they sell more than four thousand tickets to every game, they have a wait list in the thousands, and they have sold out several seasons in a row (omitting the summer of 2020, of course).

How is that possible?

The Savannah Bananas have a mantra: whatever's normal, do the exact opposite. And with this approach, they're changing how people experience baseball.

If you've ever been to a baseball game, you know they can be long, slow, and boring. (Sorry, baseball lovers.) The Bananas have gone all-in on entertainment to ensure this isn't the experience fans have at their ballpark.

Imagine being at a game with parking attendants dressed in banana costumes, a marching band welcoming you into the stadium, scratch-and-sniff tickets, all-you-can-eat meals the moment you get inside the gates (included with your ticket purchase), a break-dancing first-base coach, a senior-citizen dance team called the "Banana Nanas," players participating in skits at every half inning, batters walking to the plate on stilts. I could go on and on.

My point is, there's absolutely no way Jesse knew the Savannah Bananas would become such a popular team. What he and his team focus on are moments they can create to entertain their fans (the process, the things they can control), and the results have followed.

How far are they willing to go to entertain their fans? Well, on June 26, 2020, they played the first-ever game of Banana Ball, which is baseball with a whole new spin. Jesse explained,

> No one leaves a great movie in the middle of the movie. No one leaves a great concert in the middle of the concert. Yet, for some reason, people leave baseball games in the middle every time. And what does that say? That, maybe the game is a little bit too long, a little bit too slow, and a little bit too boring for too many fans. So we had to change it.[5]

His team devised the following nine rules for Banana Ball:

1. **Every Inning Counts.** If you win the inning, you get a point. The first team with five points wins. The moment the home team takes the lead or three outs are recorded on the home team, the inning is over.
2. **Two-Hour Time Limit.** The game is over after two hours, unless there's a tie or if a team hasn't scored five points. (If that happens, they move along to rule number seven.)
3. **No Stepping Out.** A batter stepping out of the batter's box during an at-bat is a strike, and if they step out with two strikes, they're out.

4. **No Bunting.** A bunt or attempted bunt is an automatic out.

5. **Batters Can Steal First.** If a pass ball or wild pitch occurs during an at-bat, regardless of the pitch count, the batter can attempt to run to first base.

6. **No Walks Allowed.** After four balls are pitched, the batter takes off in a sprint around the bases. The catcher must throw the ball to every defensive player on the field before the ball is live, while the batter advances to as many bases as he can.

7. **One-on-One Showdown Tiebreaker.** This is a kind of penalty-kick situation. Each team selects one pitcher and one hitter to face off. All the other players leave the field, aside from the catcher. If the pitcher strikes out the batter, his team wins. If the batter hits the ball into the field of play, the pitcher has to retrieve the ball and then either tag the batter himself or throw the ball to the catcher to tag the batter out before he crosses home plate.

8. **No Mound Visits.** No one is allowed to visit the pitcher's mound to talk to the pitcher during the game. It's simply a delay for the fans, and no one has time for that.

9. **If a Fan Catches a Foul Ball, It's an Out.** Fans now have the opportunity to be part of the game from the stands, because a fan catching a foul creates an official out on the scorecard.

Every morning Jesse creates a list of ten new ideas (the process), and he has repeated this ritual for several years now. Banana Ball was one of those simple ideas he and his team have executed to improve the fan experience. It's what he obsesses over. He can't control the number of fans that show up to the ballpark (the result), but he's learned to fall in love with the

SUCCESS IS IN THE *PROCESS,* NOT THE RESULT.

TIM SCHURRER

work of entertaining them. That process is his success. And it's a great one.

THE WAY OF THE AMATEUR

My friend Annie F. Downs wrote a terrific book titled *That Sounds Fun*.[6] In one of my favorite chapters of her book, she highlighted a definition of the word *amateur* that most people have forgotten. She explained that when we hear the word used, it's typically to describe someone not doing something very well. It's synonymous with lacking proficiency. But there's another definition, and ironically it's the first definition listed in the dictionary: "One who engages in a pursuit, study, science, or sport as a pastime rather than as a profession."[7] To put it another way: someone who does something for the love of the activity, not the money.

Gallup Inc. is one of the world's leading research firms when it comes to knowledge about the workplace. In a recent poll, they discovered that of the billion full-time workers around the globe, only 15 percent are engaged in their work.[8]

Based on this statistic, it's fair to say, most people probably don't even like their work. No wonder people aren't fulfilled by their day-to-day. They've lost the enjoyment of it or perhaps never enjoyed it in the first place. This is the exact opposite of our definition of an amateur.

COMMITTING TO THE MINDSET SHIFT

I wish more people enjoyed their work, but I know how challenging that can be. Some people are busting it to provide for their families, and they don't feel as though they have the luxury to enjoy it. Many people are forced to work jobs they hate out of economic necessity. The idea that "enjoying work is a privilege" has its merits.

If you remove the Savannah Bananas brand and their fan experience and look at the specific roles some of their staffers play every night, they don't seem to be the most enjoyable: parking attendant, ticket taker, custodial, and concessions. You could imagine how these wouldn't be considered dream jobs or anything even close to that. They'd simply be showing up for a paycheck. There's a lesson for us here, though, in how the Bananas staff have chosen to approach their work. They have decided—an intentional mindset shift—to make their jobs fun.

You may not have control over your job, but you have control over how you show up. Are you going to come into the office today with a bad attitude and let it impact you and those around you? Will you go home at the end of your shift talking about how miserable your day was (again) and how much you hate your job? Are you going to obsess about how much you dislike your career and let that consume you?

There's another way. Jesse Cole and the Savannah Bananas simply choose fun. They don't have to, but they do. You throw a banana costume on a ticket taker and show them the impact they're having on the fan experience, and the boring job of taking tickets becomes a little more enjoyable. A smile may even appear on that team member's face, and it impacts not only that person's day but also every fan they interact with. A ripple effect follows, expanding beyond anything we can measure.

The Savannah Bananas staff have decided to obsess over their customers and their experience at the ballpark. The staff spend less time focused on themselves and their needs and more time thinking about the customers and their needs. A mentality of service gives the staff a purpose for showing up, and that leads to enjoyment, even in the more difficult, boring positions at the stadium.

You might not be able to wear a banana costume to work, but you can do something. What small steps can you take toward enjoying your work more today than you did yesterday? How can you make your coworker or customer smile? Perhaps for you, enjoying your job is how you would define success, and each idea I've mentioned is simply a lead measure to that lag measure.

You can't control the result, but you can commit to the process. And attempt to live one enjoyable day at a time.

THE JOY IS IN THE JOURNEY

Would you do your job for free? I realize we all have bills to pay, but what if all that was taken care of? Would you be content with the work as your reward?

When I was working at Apple, I heard Steve Jobs say, "The joy is in the journey," and I scoffed. I laughed.

I was in a fragile place in my life when I heard those words— that is, in the final days of the season when I was trying to be a musician. I had started working at Apple, but that was mostly because I had gotten married and needed a job with a consistent paycheck. I was playing music at restaurants on the side and holding out hope that I could be a career musician, even if there was only a small chance of that happening. I was struggling while grieving the loss of my dream, and I was not enjoying the journey.

Hearing my boss say "The joy is in the journey" didn't sit well with me. *Easy for you to say*, I thought. While Steve was living his dream life, I wasn't, and I wasn't in the right headspace to hear it.

But looking back, I see that he was right. I just hadn't understood the secret. Falling in love with the work itself was the key to feeling that joy. And when we're able to focus on the process and find joy in it, we might find engaging in our day-to-day to be less of a burden.

HITTING THE BESTSELLER LIST

Fast forward to when I started working with Donald Miller. Don had written a book titled *Scary Close*, and the entire team rallied together to create a compelling book launch plan.[9] We hoped it'd do well, meaning we hoped it would sell a lot of copies and make the bestseller list. But those lists can be finicky and political, and you just never know.

A week and a half after the book's release, we were in the office when Don received a call from his publisher. We knew this was the call where he'd find out if we hit the bestseller list.

After Don took the call, he looked at us and smiled. We hit number five on the *New York Times* bestseller list. This was a huge deal. It was the highest any of his books had ever been on the list.

As you can imagine, we were elated. We exchanged high fives, we hugged, we offered our congratulations to one another. But then something beautiful happened after a few minutes of celebrating: we all went back to work.

It's said that Stephen King has a similar approach after finishing a manuscript. He'll pull the last page from the typewriter and place the manuscript in a drawer. He'll then load a fresh piece of paper into the typewriter—page one of his next book. This is a man in love with the work, not the result or the external validation.

That's why I thought our response to *Scary Close* hitting the *New York Times* bestseller list was so special. We weren't in it solely to hit the list. It's a nice bit of validation for the hard work we had put in, but it wasn't our "why." I would have been just as content having done the work without that badge, and I think that's true of others on the team as well. And we didn't celebrate, not because we were dysfunctional. We acknowledged the win; we just weren't caught up in it. I was going to show up at work the same way the next day, no matter how well the book did. For me, that was a sign of personal growth. I was happy to be a part of the project, regardless of the outcome.

The work was the reward.

SUCCESS IS IN THE PROCESS

As I look back on my journey of wanting to be a full-time musician so badly, of wanting to be the next John Mayer, I wonder if one of the reasons this didn't work out was because I was trying to become a professional too soon.

I wonder what would have happened on this journey if I had let myself be an amateur for a while. I wonder what would have happened if I had fallen in love with songwriting and production. If I had given myself permission to travel and play shows, and not have made the number of people showing up or the amount of merchandise I sold to be my primary markers of success. If I had just enjoyed the journey and said, "If music turns into something career-wise, great! But if not, that's fine too." I should have been content with the process and not have tied my happiness so tightly to the result.

Maybe you are where I was and just don't believe the joy is in the journey. Perhaps things haven't played out for you in your life like you thought they would, and it sure doesn't seem like a realistic possibility. Or maybe you're trying out different jobs or feeling restless in the one you have.

My hope for you is that you can find something soon where you can say "the joy is in the journey" and mean it. Where you're not motivated by the money or the accolades but by the work itself. Where you focus on the process, surrender the outcome, and let the results take care of themselves.

Success is in the process, not the result.

WHAT'S THE POINT
— OF DOING —
ANYTHING *if* IT'S EASY?
IT'S SO MUCH MORE
VALUABLE WHEN A
CHALLENGE HAS *to* BE
OVERCOME.

SCOTT HAMILTON

EMBRACE CHALLENGES AND **LEARN** FROM **FAILURE**

If I told you to draw a line that modeled what a successful career looked like, what would you draw? My guess is you'd draw something like this:

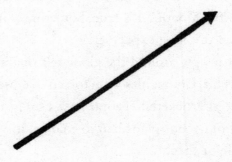

We want our career lines to look like healthy growth. In fact, professional résumé builders coach us to show progress on our résumés, with each move showing a promotion or added responsibility. If there's a perceived lateral move or a gap or a step back, that isn't good. We'd have to explain it and show how the transition was actually positive. This type of advice is given because of the way most businesspeople interpret career moves.

I used to think my path to success, my version of climbing the ladder, would look like a steady progression. I thought my career would be a slow climb to the top, without any major hurdles. Perhaps when I reached my fifties, which I perceived as my peak, I would look back and feel proud of all I had accomplished. And, being not too far from retirement, I would use my final decade to leave a legacy and mentor others before resigning to my new life, where I would most certainly be at a golf course several days a week.

This image for my life missed one key ingredient: life is full of unexpected, disorienting, and difficult situations.

We regularly experience all kinds of setbacks. A career that is less fulfilling than we dreamed it would be. A business partner flying off the rails. A flood of stress and anxiety due to the added responsibilities of a new position.

The boxer Mike Tyson said, "Everyone has a plan until they get punched in the mouth." It's true. Sometimes life gives you a right hook when you least expect it.

Millions of people around the globe felt this in 2020, when the coronavirus hit. Companies were forced to close their offices. Unemployment skyrocketed. People lost family members and friends. For all of us, our plans had to change. It was a punch to the face we didn't expect.

I knew in theory that life could deal me unplanned twists and turns, and yet I never imagined I'd experience any real challenges. My recipe for success lacked any kind of challenge awareness. I don't think I'm alone in this. Many of us want and expect our journey to go nicely on a résumé. No explanations needed. But if you've been trying something for more than five seconds, my guess is you know the truth: sooner or later hardship will come, ready or not.

The actual drawing of success looks more like this:

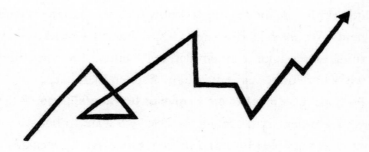

Real life is full of punches to the face, circumstances beyond our control that knock us down and backward and send us reeling. A client you're working with has a bad experience with you and writes a formal complaint. You don't make the sale you wanted to make. Your boss quits. You get laid off. You get pregnant when you're not trying to. You don't get pregnant when you *are* trying to. Someone in your family gets sick. We get frustrated when our experiences don't match the steady incline we expect.

Where does this idea of a career without challenges come from?

- **It's not from movies.** Those are chock-full of challenges for the main character to overcome. In fact, in the latest blockbuster, I would bet you anything a major challenge comes at the protagonist within the first ten minutes.
- **It's not from real life.** If you're breathing, you experience challenges each and every day; sometimes big, sometimes small, but problems nonetheless.

- **Perhaps it's influenced by popular culture.** We are exposed to dozens of celebrities and influencers, and because of social media, we get to see more of their lives than ever before. What we don't hear much about is what a lot of these people had to overcome to get where they are. For every overnight success, there are many more multiple-decade successes. I don't think anyone wants to know how the sausage is truly made. We see celebrities and CEOs, and it seems like everything worked out for them without a hitch. And sometimes we believe our lives can actually happen like that.
- **Perhaps it's a mechanism to give us (or others) hope.** When we see others experiencing success, we want to believe the same is possible for us and those we love. And, especially if we're not all that happy with our lives, dreaming of a better life is an escape.

But a successful career without hardships or challenges? That just doesn't exist.

If children say they want to be a firefighter, we say, "That's awesome!" We don't tell them how difficult that career is. Imagine telling your son or daughter, "You want to be a firefighter when you grow up? Well, there are a few things you should know. It's one of the most demanding certifications you can get. And I'm not sure if you've thought about the physical and emotional strain this job takes. You'll push your body to the limits putting out those fires, often risking your own safety. Not only that, firefighters regularly experience loss, which will require counseling and other support to keep you in a good headspace throughout your career." Of course we don't tell kids about the realities like this when they're young.

But at what point would it be helpful for them to know the truth? While the challenges in every profession are real, people don't often get that honest about them.

Regardless of how I arrived at the wild narrative that my successful career would be without hurdles, I'm learning the reality now. I solve problems each and every day, some of which are extremely challenging and more than I can bear on my own at times. While there are moments when I wish these things would all go away, I have to wonder, *Would my life be all that interesting if there were no challenges?*

THE CHALLENGE MAKES THE STORY

Even more than being unrealistic, the idea that our lives would just go as planned—up, up, up—makes for a boring life. Is a life void of failure or any real challenges even worth pursuing?

One of my favorite books is Donald Miller's *A Million Miles in a Thousand Years*. I read it in a single sitting (from 10:00 p.m. to 4:00 a.m.). I couldn't put it down! Since that night in 2009, my life has never been the same. The book starts by teaching the basic elements of a story. What is a good story all about? The definition Don gives is this: "A character who wants something and overcomes conflict to get it."[1] The problems in the story start quickly, and pretty soon the audience is rooting for the protagonist to win the day.

If there's one thing I learned from almost a decade working alongside Don, it's that good stories are not void of conflict. In fact, without a problem or challenge to overcome, there is no story at all. Movies are full of twists and turns, as we watch how the main characters try to overcome all that's thrown at them. The challenges make the story interesting, and they ultimately make the story meaningful.

What if the same is true in our lives as well? What if, instead of problems ruining our stories, they actually make them better? What if challenges make our stories more interesting and meaningful?

Think about what it would be like if everything worked out for you. You were born into a wealthy family, your parents gave you a brand-new BMW as your first car, you were accepted into a prestigious university, your grades were nothing but As, you secured the first job you applied for and were offered more money than you even asked for in the interview. Not only that, but you didn't have any debt, and you married the first person you were in a relationship with.

Now imagine if someone made a movie about your life. Would anyone be interested in watching it?

Challenges don't take away from our stories; they make them. Challenges help us identify what we want in life. Challenges make us grateful. Challenges reveal our need to learn and develop. Challenges allow us to see how strong we are. Challenges show us who we can rely on and who we can't. Challenges deepen our empathy for others. Challenges put our priorities in order. Challenges keep us humble.

Without challenges, our lives aren't that deep, that rich, or that interesting.

But that's not how we act. Perhaps we feel pressure to have it all together. And when we combine that with a rose-colored lens about celebrity success stories and a tendency to ignore reality, we resist hardship like it's a sign of failure. This is the influence of the Spotlight Mindset. We feel we have to be perfect, ready for all eyes to be on us, obsessed with how we appear. We don't allow for mistakes. We want our success to look natural and effortless.

What if we stopped trying to avoid challenges, stopped trying to pretend they weren't there, or stopped trying to edit them out of our lives completely? How, then, might we deal with challenges?

LEARNING TO FALL

There are few people who know more about failure and hardship than Olympic figure skater Scott Hamilton.

He is famously known for his backflip, which he performs regularly in exhibitions to light up the crowd. He's also known for his gold-medal win at the 1984 Winter Olympics. But what you might not know about Scott is that he was adopted at a young age when his biological mother decided she couldn't take care of him. He also didn't grow as quickly as other kids because of a childhood illness, and so he was smaller than the skaters he competed against. His adopted mom, whom he loved dearly, died of cancer when he was a teenager. At one point in his life, a judge made it very clear to Scott that he didn't stand a chance as a competitive figure skater. And, if that weren't enough, he has fought and survived cancer and three brain tumors.

So if anyone knows what it means to get the short end of the stick, it's Scott. But he has never seen his challenges as disadvantages. He's always seen them as opportunities to help him get to where he's trying to go. He has even gone as far as to call them blessings.[2] And he's being genuine!

Scott now runs a world-class skating school in Nashville,

where athletes come to get better at their craft. When the students arrive at the Scott Hamilton Skating Academy, they want to learn how to do what Scott does; namely, they want to learn how to do a backflip (among other jumps). But to learn how to do what Scott does, they have to learn how to fail. They have to learn how to *fall*.

If you have followed Scott's career even tangentially, you probably know about his winning performance at the Olympics. It included an impressive jump sequence: triple lutz, triple toe loop, triple flip, triple toe Walley, triple Salchow. He landed three of the five.[3] And even without landing them all, he walked away with a gold medal. Scott knows the truth about failure that I wish all of us knew: embracing failure will help you win.

It's no surprise that Scott's students want to learn the same jumps that led to his prolific figure-skating career. I wonder how many of them are disappointed when they find out they'll be starting with something a bit different. The first thing Scott and his instructors teach is how to fall. Every student, no matter how old or what skill level they are at, starts with the basics. Because Scott knows, no matter how good you are, if you're working toward success as a figure skater, sooner or later you're going to hit the ice. Falling safely and getting back up are important foundational skills, because falling is a life guarantee.

The idea that a notable career (the ability to skate or any other worthwhile endeavor) looks like a steady incline to the top is ridiculous. If we're not going to avoid, ignore, or hide our problems, we need a completely different approach.

The Secret Society has taught me that a successful career looks like embracing challenges and learning from failure.

EMBRACE CHALLENGES

It's not our natural instinct to embrace challenges.

Experts divide our instinctual responses to trauma into three basic categories: fight, flight, or freeze. When we encounter even minor challenges, our natural instinct is to face our challenges (fight), avoid them (flight), or, in a paralyzed panic, do nothing (freeze). Any of these tactics might be helpful in extreme circumstances too: fight the wild animal, flee from the wild animal, or hide from the wild animal. Do one of those and you might make it out alive.

But when it comes to our everyday challenges, *flight* and *freeze* rarely work out in the long run. While sometimes these tactics successfully deter hardships in the short term, they tend to make our problems worse.

It'd be difficult to work with someone who gets overwhelmed when they're up against challenges. Someone who throws up their hands and says, "I don't know what to do! I give up!" That's a *freeze* mentality. It's natural, but it's not helpful.

Working with someone with a *flight* mentality is even worse. In a business environment, it might look like continuing on as normal while simultaneously allowing the company to slowly burn to the ground. It could also look like denial and continuing practices that everyone knows don't work.

Every business faced challenges in 2020. Many fought and didn't survive. But the ones that had the best chance of survival were not the ones that *froze* or *fled*. Giving up at the outset ruined their chances from the start. Those that denied the situation failed to adapt in time and that shot them in the foot as well.

Throughout 2020, successful leadership recognized the

challenges at hand but also found a way forward. "We can do it." "We can fight this." "Let's pivot." "Let's shift our messaging." "Let's do what we need to do to come out stronger on the other side." That's a *fight* mentality.

When firefighters see a challenge, when they spot a fire, they run toward it. They don't expect anyone else to put out the fire. They don't wait for it to die out. They don't pretend they don't see smoke. They have trained for this moment, and so when they see a fire, they immediately go toward it. They see the problem and they embrace it.

It's easy to see how a *fight* mentality contributes to a productive team. You want to work alongside people who are willing to engage in whatever challenge you are up against. A dream colleague is the person who says, "I'm in. What's the problem? Whatever it takes, let's get into it." Somebody who's willing to fight is somebody who's willing to see a challenge for what it is, and then figure out what they need to do or the person they need to be to rise to that challenge.

The further I get into my career, the more I want to be like a firefighter. I want to see fire and smoke as opportunities to embrace challenges, as I know this is the path to a meaningful life. To adopt this approach is the way of the Secret Society. You might not be at that place now, but I hope by the end of this book you'll want to be that kind of person too.

Challenges don't have to be the enemy; they don't have to be wasted or pointless experiences. Think of working out. That's a regular practice where we intentionally put ourselves through discomfort so we can grow. While we might not enjoy the difficulty of the workout, we know it's making us stronger. It's building muscle.

I'm not suggesting we intentionally bring painful situations into our careers. But if we know anything about life, it's that challenges will come whether we want them to or not.

In your career, you will experience hardships. How will you choose to view them? Will you see that time as wasted or shameful? Will you say, "That experience knocked me down"? Or will you learn from those struggles? Will you see those experiences as part of what makes you better? Will you say, "What broke me down made me stronger"?

If you think you can have a life without challenges, it might be time to name that vision as the fantasy it is. It's not possible to live an interesting, meaningful life without challenges. And if you want to have a successful career, you need to start by embracing challenges as your pathway there.

LEARN FROM FAILURE

The moment I threw hundreds of my own CDs into a dumpster humbled me. As a musician, I had ordered thousands of copies of my music as inventory to sell. I worked hard to book venues and put every detail of every show together. I would walk into those venues expecting the room to be full, but the place would be practically empty. And when people did come, it didn't mean they'd buy my albums. After years of not selling them, I didn't have much of a choice but to get rid of the merchandise that was taking up space in my garage.

It felt unfair. I felt like I deserved better. I felt like I'd failed. I felt like a victim. My expectation that my career would be a straight line "up and to the right" only left me frustrated.

Today I realize all the highs and lows in my career have set me up to do exactly what I'm doing now. They gave me empathy for anyone trying to build something from the ground up. I learned about my aptitude for rallying a team of people around an idea and bringing that idea to life.

As I transitioned from wanting to be a musician to working alongside a musician as a manager, I saw a new path for myself, one in which I could be a part of the creative side, but in a position where I could own the logistics and operations parts of the project. Those skills—both supporting creatives and managing huge projects—equipped me for my role in leading the team at StoryBrand. If I had not failed as a musician, I don't think those other things would have been possible.

Every failure is an opportunity to learn. Scott Hamilton said, "No matter who you are and no matter what finishing first looks like for you, any goal will always have obstacles, difficulties, and setbacks. You will be defined not by those setbacks but by how you respond to them."[4] Let your response be an attitude of curiosity.

Professional golfer Ben Crane exemplifies this well. Instead of focusing on failure, he leads himself through three reflection questions after every round of golf.

1. What did I do well?
2. What did I learn?
3. How can I act on what I learned?

The second question gets at the heart of failure. Instead of asking what went wrong, the question prompts a positive response: What's the learning here?

Ben's three questions align with a philosophy articulated by Olympic sports shooter Lanny Bassham, author of *With Winning in Mind*.[5] His philosophy is that you move toward what you focus on. So if you focus on failure, you are more likely to fail. You set yourself up to repeat those same mistakes. But if you focus on success, you will be more likely to succeed.

Ben has adopted the Mental Management System, which was created by Lanny. Instead of fixating on the negative, Ben asks himself what he learned. This question frames even his failures as paths to success. He doesn't list negatives; he lists *lessons*. Ben said, "There're no mistakes, it's just learning. It's just an OTE [opportunity to excel] with our learning and to make corrections."[6] This framing leaves a positive impression on the brain, rather than a negative one. Then the third question takes him to action: How will you respond?

Scott Hamilton was right. Your *response* defines you way more than your failures.

KEEP MOVING FORWARD

On the show *Ted Lasso*, actor Jason Sudeikis plays Ted Lasso, an American who steps in to coach a British football (soccer) team. In one episode, to motivate one of his players, he said, "You know what the happiest animal in the world is? It's a goldfish. It's got a ten-second memory. Be a goldfish."

Whether we're an athlete or an actor playing an athlete or in any other profession, Ted Lasso is on to something here. We must learn to move past our perceived failures and keep pushing. Instead of being weighed down by the past, keep your memory of failures short and keep moving forward.

Scott Hamilton personifies this "keep moving forward" principle. When he was about two years old, he experienced a mysterious illness that kept him from growing. For the next six years, his doctors gave him a series of improper treatments. It was determined he had cystic fibrosis (which was inaccurate), and he was told he had six months to live (again, inaccurate). His parents then took him to the Boston Children's Hospital, where he was given a new treatment of diet and exercise, and he started showing health improvements and began growing again. Even though he'd always be smaller than his peers (today, he stands at five feet, four inches), he was in good health just a year after arriving at Boston Children's. It was around this time that he convinced his parents to let him skate. Being on the ice was an escape for Scott. And, well, the rest is history.

Although Scott's story is incredible, he doesn't consider his journey to be unrelatable. He said,

> You don't have to be diagnosed with a life-threatening illness to uncover your own inner resilience. All you need is to know what you truly desire, what you want badly enough that you're willing to do anything to get it. Then you begin to deal with the obstacles and "limitations" getting in your way—and decide that you're finished with letting anything keep you from living the life you want to live.[7]

Notice his encouragement to focus on what you desire. Instead of letting so-called limitations keep you down, you must keep moving forward.

It's curious how many people are caught off guard when hard times come. It could be their health, their relationships, or their career. Challenges will come, but they don't have to throw you off course. They don't have to hold you back. The Secret Society has taught me that failure is a stepping-stone to something more. Focus on what you're learning (Ben Crane's

CHALLENGES ARE **PART OF THE JOURNEY** TO SUCCESS. IN FACT, EXPERIENCING FAILURE AND **LEARNING FROM IT** IS THE FASTEST WAY TO ACHIEVE YOUR GOALS.

TIM SCHURRER

reflection questions), and allow every step to propel you to the next challenge.

HOW TOMS TURNED FAILURE
INTO FORWARD MOTION

Imagine ordering thirty thousand units when you meant to order three thousand. You don't need to know what's being ordered to know that this mistake of an extra zero is a big one.

For TOMS, the order was for white canvas shoes.[8] And because it was a special order (no one else was making shoes like this at the time), they couldn't return them. As we saw in chapter 6, the company is known for soft canvas-style slip-ons and for making a splash with their one-for-one business model. But this mistake happened in their second year of business, before TOMS hit its peak popularity, and it could have ended them. What were they going to do with all these white canvas shoes?

One strategy would be to take the hit and mark down all the merchandise to sell as much as possible. But TOMS didn't believe that was the right decision when trying to build the brand long term. Instead, company founder Blake Mycoskie used this moment as an OTE (opportunity to excel). Rather than run from this moment of challenge and perceived failure, he embraced it. He gathered his team, and they came up with an idea: bring in Tyler Ramsey, an artist specializing in Jackson Pollock–style art, to paint the shoes.

Their customers loved it. Soon TOMS couldn't produce the hand-painted shoes fast enough to keep them in stock on their website. They had to suspend Tyler from a forklift and line the floor beneath him with thousands of shoes so he could splatter large quantities all at once. To date, Tyler has painted more than 120,000 shoes.

And that good idea sparked another. Instead of only selling "art pieces" by Tyler Ramsey, TOMS pitched the shoes as a blank canvas for customers to create their own expression, and started hosting events called "Style Your Sole," where anyone could paint their own shoes. This is where my life intersected with TOMS.

I was in college when I first heard about TOMS and their one-for-one model. I bought some of their shoes, but I wanted to do more and be a part of this movement somehow. An opportunity opened up for me to move to Santa Monica and work at the TOMS headquarters for a season, so I jumped on it.

While in California, I joined the team that booked Style Your Sole events at colleges all over the country. After we had all the events on the calendar for the fall, we jumped into fifteen-passenger vans and set out. Being on the ground with TOMS fans and customers and seeing the passion in each of them was something I'll never forget.

It was the relentless optimism of the team at HQ that made all this possible, though. They didn't buy into the myth of the slow rise to the top without any negative turns. They *fought* and created an opportunity out of a potentially tragic mistake. They learned what they needed to learn and kept moving forward.

The decisions of Blake and his team have impacted my life too. If they didn't choose to face the extra-zero ordering blunder head-on, I might never have experienced working for the company, and who knows how that would have changed my path.

When people are stuck in a Spotlight Mindset, experiencing failure is something they don't want any part of. They are so concerned with how others perceive them that to be seen as anything but a success would destroy their ego.

It's vulnerable to face challenges. It's humbling to fail. Those with a Spotlight Mindset would rather cover up their mistakes and hardships than embrace them.

What I've discovered is that challenges are part of the journey to success. In fact, experiencing failure and learning from it is the fastest way to achieve your goals. Scott Hamilton taught me, "The goal isn't to begin failing less but to learn how to be better at facing failure, so we can leverage our failures as our best opportunities to learn."[9] Challenges are always up ahead, and we have to get good at running toward them.

Remember, the way of the Secret Society is to be a firefighter.

THERE IS
NO LIMIT
TO WHAT A MAN
CAN DO OR WHERE
HE CAN GO IF
HE DOESN'T MIND
WHO GETS THE
CREDIT.

FROM A PLAQUE
THAT SAT ON

RONALD REAGAN'S

DESK DURING
HIS PRESIDENCY

10

WHEN
YOU DON'T MIND WHO
GETS THE CREDIT

Imagine making decisions that impact millions of people and not actually getting credit for your work.

Alyssa Mastromonaco was White House deputy chief of staff for operations from 2011 to 2014 under President Barack Obama, the youngest person to ever hold the position. She worked closely with Obama for a decade, starting with his senate campaign and continuing into his presidency. She'd become his right hand. Not much happened in Obama's world that she didn't know about or contribute to in some way.

She was responsible for the entire eighteen-acre White House compound and the more than seventeen hundred employees in the executive branch.[1] Not only this, she oversaw the thirty-five hundred members of the military that support Air Force One, Camp David, and Marine One.[2] In her book *Who Thought This Was a Good Idea?*, she described her position:

At any high-powered job, you're going to have to work a lot. America is a nation of people who work a lot and of people who strive to work a lot. The best thing you can be, our culture tells us, is "at the top of your field." You are supposed to want to have power, to be an executive with a cushy corner office and a lot of money and an assistant, a person who travels for business and takes working breakfasts, fork in one hand and cell phone in the other. When I worked at the White House, this was my life, minus the corner office and the large quantity of money, but with the added bonus of being able to do something I really loved for causes that I really believed in, with people who taught me something new every day, if not every hour.[3]

When I look at Alyssa's work alongside Obama, I see a Secret Society member with strong internal motivation and passion for her work. She worked long hours and led teams of people and projects that impacted all Americans, as well as the world at large, but she didn't need the credit for it. That's not what she cared about. That's not what motivated her.

So much of what the president accomplished during those years was possible because of her work. And yet Alyssa Mastromonaco's name is almost unknown. She didn't demand the spotlight and, in fact, was willing to give the president the credit for what she contributed. "I attribute a lot of my success to never losing sight of the fact that I worked for Barack Obama," she said. "I was not Barack Obama. I am never going to be Barack Obama."[4] And her ability to pass along the credit, she seemed to say, helped her to succeed.

I think she's on to something.

A CHANGE YOU'LL EXPERIENCE IN YOURSELF

As you progress in the way of the Secret Society, you'll start to notice a change in yourself. You don't need the attention quite as badly as you used to. What once felt all-consuming—the chase for more or what's next—doesn't take up much of your mental bandwidth anymore. These days you are motivated by your contribution to the team and how you are helping others around you win. You used to wait anxiously to be called out in meetings or recognized by your boss. You used to complain when you felt unnoticed or underappreciated. Now you don't stress about it. You go to work mostly thinking about the task at hand.

Isn't it a good feeling?

If you find yourself in this spot, you're getting it. In fact, you're getting to an advanced level. Not only are you aware of the destruction the Spotlight Mindset can bring, but you've also come to focus on what the Secret Society cares about.

If you're not there, don't worry. It can take several reps to get to this spot. This attitude describes someone who has been training in the way of the Secret Society for a long time. If you're just starting out, don't beat yourself up for not yet feeling this way. It will happen with time.

For those of you who are seeing this change in yourself, I predict you're going to get recognized soon. Someone is going to pat you on the back or give you credit for your work. Someone's going to acknowledge you, which is something you may have desperately wanted before, but you're not going to know what to do with it.

When you first notice this internal shift, it'll feel different (at least it did for me) to receive attention for your work. Before, I would have felt deserving. *Finally*, I'd think to myself. Like a car in need of gas, I'd take it in. I'd feel happy for the day. But that satisfaction would not last. *What about everything else I was doing?*

But now, when praise comes, it feels like a nice surprise more than anything else. Icing on the cake. I appreciate it, but it's not why I come into work. Attention and recognition are no longer my fuel to keep going. I'm already full with everything I need.

So what does a Secret Society member do when faced with this nice surprise? It's just as revolutionary and countercultural as the rest of their actions: they give away the credit.

"I DON'T THINK ABOUT MYSELF THAT MUCH"

When someone gives the credit away as a knee-jerk reaction, it's a telltale sign they're part of the Secret Society.

One of my favorite examples of this comes from a man who spent most of his career in the shadows. Before becoming Apple's CEO, Tim Cook was COO under the leadership of Steve Jobs. For years, Tim worked quietly behind the scenes as the world had its eyes on Steve Jobs. For all the work Tim did, the show still revolved around Steve. The spotlight didn't move. But when Steve Jobs passed away from pancreatic cancer at age fifty-six, way earlier than anyone expected, Tim stepped up to the plate.

Tim Cook was the one Steve Jobs had been grooming for this role, and it was finally his time to step out and be seen. How does a person even begin to fill the shoes of someone as iconic and world changing as Steve Jobs?

Three and a half years into his role as CEO, Tim had a chance to show the world that he was ready to lead this company into a new era. It was time to launch the Apple Watch, which was the first new product release since Steve's passing. New versions of iPhones and iPads and computers had been released in the years leading up to this moment, but this was the first product launched in a new category under Tim's leadership.

During an interview with David Muir on *Nightline*, right after the big announcement about the Apple Watch, David asked Tim, "Is this the moment for you—the moment of your career at Apple?"

You might expect Tim to have answered as most people might have in this situation; namely, talk a bit about the journey he'd been on to arrive there. He'd been working diligently under the radar for years. People didn't know how much he had contributed to Apple's success, and this was an opportunity to hint at or even come out and say directly all he'd done to be standing where he was. This was his opportunity to get a little credit.

But Tim's response went in the opposite direction: "Well, it's a moment for Apple. I don't really think about myself that much."[5] Those two sentences reveal everything you need to know about Tim and the way he leads.

On a world stage, in a nationally televised interview before millions of viewers, he did not take the bait. He decided this was not the Tim Cook show. He saw himself as a team member. Instead of looking for credit, he gave the credit away.

That is inspirational to me, because I know I'm not there yet. If I had been on a world stage like that, I'd be so tempted to revel in the spotlight. Tim Cook showed me I still have some work to do.

His response reminded me of a plaque that sat on President Reagan's desk while he was in the White House: "There is no limit to what a man can do or where he can go if he doesn't mind who gets the credit."[6] Tim Cook gave away the credit, which is what good leaders do. They lift up those who do the behind-the-scenes work. It's a conscious decision, and I see it as a mark of not only a good leader but of a quality person.

Even though we may not be on a world stage, you and I have opportunities to do what Tim Cook modeled for us. If your boss calls you out during a meeting for doing good work, share the credit. If someone singles you out, point them to your team.

DEFLECTING VS. SHARING CREDIT

I want to pause to make an important distinction here between deflecting credit and sharing credit. Have you ever had a moment when someone appreciated you, and you didn't know how to take the compliment? I'm sure this has happened to most of us. We get nervous, we don't know where to look, or we start fidgeting. Then we do what feels natural in the moment: we deflect. We say, "I didn't do that much" or "It really was nothing," when actually we did a lot, and it really took quite some time.

Here's the catch. Needing credit and deflecting credit stem from the same root: insecurity. We either need credit because we don't feel worthy unless we have it, or we don't take credit because we don't feel worthy. Each of these seemingly opposite attitudes have the same problem: lack of confidence or self-worth.

The practice I've been describing is less about not taking credit and more about an attitude of not needing it. The fact that we don't need credit comes from a place of knowing our own worth and knowing the value of our work. It comes from believing in oneself. If we know the value of what we've done, we can confidently accept appreciation and graciously include others.

The truth is, none of us have gotten where we are today

without some help, guidance, and support. As John Donne accurately articulated in 1624: "No man is an island, entire of itself; every man is a piece of the continent, a part of the main."[7] We are not alone, and most of what we do in a day is a team effort in one way or another.

More than that, not needing credit comes from a posture of gratitude. For me, being a parent is what taught me this lesson.

"ISN'T IT AN HONOR?"

Parenting can be difficult at times. It demands patience and presence even when all you want to do is take a nap. And there's no real break. Even though people tried to prepare me for what parenting was going to be like, I didn't fully understand what they were telling me until I was in it. But, you know, I didn't get into this whole parenting thing for my life to get easier. No one looks at their partner and says, "I think we should start a family. It'll make our lives really easy and less complicated." While I knew there would be innumerable challenges, there's something about it I was drawn to. My wife and I were up for the adventure in spite of all we didn't know.

On the days when I am stretched to the max, when I'm physically exhausted and mentally worn out by the constant demands of mediating and feeding and playing and mediating (yep, twice) and I don't think I can push through, I have to find a way to dig deep and keep showing up. It's on those days when your mindset and your actions are challenged that you have to decide how you're going to show up. Will you respond with patience and grace and compassion? Or will you respond in a way you won't be proud of later?

THE SECRET IS
—
FINDING THE MOTIVATION
TO **SHOW UP AT YOUR BEST,**
KNOWING YOU'LL NEVER
GET THE CREDIT YOU DESERVE FOR
DOING A JOB WELL.
—
BUT BEYOND THAT,
TO **JOYFULLY DO THE WORK**
WITHOUT EVEN NEEDING
THE CREDIT IN THE FIRST PLACE.

TIM SCHURRER

In parenting, you'll never get the credit you deserve, from people looking at what you do from the outside or even from your kids. No parent ever has or ever will.

Perhaps this is why Mother's Day and Father's Day feel more meaningful every year. Not for me and my wife, necessarily, but as I think about our parents. My friend Sarah wrote a beautiful tribute to her mom in a post this past Mother's Day that articulates the way a lot of us feel about the people who reared us:

> Sometimes when I'm rocking our son back to sleep at 2 a.m., I think about how I spent most of my life not even considering that you did the same for me. Moms are magic, and tragically it usually takes us a few decades to figure that out. With every new season or experience in motherhood, I find a new reason to say thank you. Thank you for pouring yourself out, even when we had no idea just how loved we were. I think I'm getting it now.[8]

This is the type of message I'm trying to write to my mom in her Mother's Day cards these days. Like Sarah, I didn't understand most of what my mom did for me until I experienced some of those things myself. I'm learning how special it is to have her as a mom as I try to raise two kids of my own. I may not have given her credit back then, but I'm trying to make up for it now. Not everyone has a good relationship with their parents, and not everyone gets to look back on their childhood with fond memories of how they were cared for. But I want to believe, even if things weren't perfect, that most parents were doing the best they knew how and were continually sacrificing along the way.

The secret in parenting and in life is finding the motivation to show up at your best, knowing you'll never get the credit you deserve for doing a job well. But beyond that, to joyfully do the work without even needing the credit in the first place.

I have unique opportunities to see how my wife, Katie, models this in our home. I knew she was amazing, but things went to another level after we had kids.

Recently our son was scheduled for an annual checkup. We told him about it the day before to warm him up to the idea. As soon as we told him, the look on his face changed. I thought, *This is not going to go well tomorrow.* But Katie didn't give up. She grabbed the toy doctor's kit from the toy bin and took out the plastic stethoscope and otoscope, as well as some pretend bandages and other supplies you'd find at a doctor's office.

"Hey, Judson, I see you're a little nervous about it. Do you want to practice?" she asked. "Do you want to be the doctor or the patient?"

For a full thirty minutes they took turns, and the look on his face slowly evolved from nervousness to curiosity and even to joy. These are the moments no one will ever give her credit for. The ones where she allows him to feel his feelings but guides him through those emotions in a gentle, loving way.

I asked Katie how she finds the motivation to give and give, expecting nothing in return. How she is able to keep going, knowing she'll never get the credit for all she does. She told me that a few months after Judson was born, she had been talking with another new mom about the constant demands of waking up in the middle of the night for feedings and all the other stuff that leave parents feeling exhausted. Her friend responded in a way Katie will never forget.

She said with genuine gratitude, "Isn't it an honor?"

That flipped a switch in Katie's heart and mind. She started to look at it that way—as an honor to be the one person who can always soothe, the one person who is needed and trusted so deeply. In spite of all the inherent challenges, she is committed to doing what's best for our kids, even if it makes things more difficult for her.

"That's just how I'm going to do it," she said. "Now, it's become a habit."

This is the way of the Secret Society. To put in the work without needing the credit, even if it requires self-sacrifice. Seeing the whole thing as an honor.

For so long I chased after the credit. All I wanted was to be recognized for my work. I believed that this more than anything would satisfy me. I thought I could outrun the Spotlight Mindset. I thought if I could just get a little credit, then I'd be able to give up the chase for the next thing, the climb to the top of the ladder. If I got the credit, then I would feel satisfied, and this Spotlight Mindset wouldn't have its hold on me.

But I suspect you know the truth by now, if not from these stories then from your own experience. You know that getting your fifteen minutes of fame, your highlight in the newsletter, the promotion you always wanted—none of these will satisfy the need for more. As Gertrude Stein said, "There is no there there."[9]

I used to think the more successful I became, the more credit I would get. But as I've started to live in the way of the Secret Society, and as I've found more success, I'm learning that's not how I want to live. The more successful I become, the more credit I want to give away. And not only this, I'm learning what it looks like to not need the credit in the first place.

DESIRE *is*

INFINITE.

IT HAS

NO LIMIT.

NO POINT *at* WHICH IT'S EVER

SATISFIED.

———

THE PROBLEM IS,

WE ARE FINITE;

WE HAVE ALL SORTS *of* LIMITS...

SO THE RESULT IS

RESTLESSNESS.

JOHN MARK COMER

11

WHEN IS
ENOUGH, ENOUGH?

I was on my way to the office one morning, and if I'm honest, I was completely overwhelmed. I love my job, but some days there is a lot spinning around in my brain. An unending task list. Another product to launch. A growing team. Never knowing if we're going to hit the ambitious goals we've set. Putting out another fire from an escalated customer service interaction. A long list of emails to respond to. It can start to feel like too much.

So I was trying to get myself in a good headspace by listening to a podcast. I do this most mornings during my commute, but I'm convinced the episode I stumbled on wasn't an accident. The message that morning was by Jason Strand, a pastor at Eagle Brook Church in Minneapolis. He brought up one of the most famous psalms about a shepherd watching over his sheep as they grazed in green pastures. And he really got my attention when he brought up a phenomenon I'd never heard of: sheep bloating.[1]

Unless you've lived on a farm, my guess is you haven't heard of it either. Sheep, apparently, when left to their own devices, don't know when to stop eating. They don't know when they've had enough or too much. So as they're feeding in the fields, it's not uncommon for them to eat way too much grass, which can cause them to get really sick or even die.[2] The crazy part is that you would think they would die from eating something unhealthy or poisonous. But with bloating, this is not the case; they actually die from eating really healthy food. Green pastures are all around them, but if they don't stop eating, it can kill them.

The subject of Jason's message was how tired we are as a society. How the pressure we feel to go fast, do more, and work harder is becoming dangerous. To me it was clear. Jason was talking about the Spotlight Mindset. The Spotlight Mindset is always prompting us to chase after more. And there's always more out there to chase: more money, more influence, more attention. There are opportunities everywhere. The problem is, overconsumption can be really dangerous. As we strive, we have to realize there are consequences to chasing after more.

What I learned from Jason's podcast episode was that the role of a shepherd isn't just to keep the animals safe from predators and move them from grazing grounds to grazing grounds; it's also to keep them from overeating. If a sheep doesn't show restraint, the shepherd's job is to intervene and make them lie down, forcing them to stop eating. This brings a whole new meaning to the well-known psalm: "The LORD is my shepherd, I lack nothing. He makes me lie down in green pastures."[3]

Jason brought his message home: "You can lie down or you can be pushed down. You can slow down or you can fall down."

Maybe you're tired. Maybe you're overwhelmed. Maybe you're

exhausted from all the striving. And maybe it's not because there's something wrong. You likely have green pastures all around you. There's so much you could do or accomplish, and the allure of money, fame, and power draws you in.

So the question is this: Are you going to lie down? Are you going to find satisfaction and contentment where you are and learn to define success for yourself? Or are you going to keep chasing—despite the warning signs, despite the cost—and choose the Spotlight Mindset? If so, what will it take to wake you up? A health crisis, a divorce, a massive failure, a leadership crash? When will you see that enough is enough?

THE DANGER OF MORE, MORE, MORE

When I'm stuck in the Spotlight Mindset, I find myself exhausted and worried about what the stress from this way of approaching my life and career will do to me physically. I'm no doctor, but I know enough to realize I could be setting myself up for a heart attack or mental health problems.

It's times such as these when I think to myself, *Is this worth it? Are the scoreboards worth my health and quality of life? Is the constant drive for a little more attention and recognition worth the anxiety, the constant stress, the overwhelm?*

I've seen it in others, and at times I worry for myself whether it's only a matter of time before I crash too, if not physically, perhaps emotionally. Even when we're doing really well on the outside, sometimes what suffers are the things that matter most to us.

When Michael Hyatt secured his dream job as general manager for Nelson Books, the division was, in his words, "dead last in every significant financial metric. It was losing money, it wasn't growing, the morale of the team was terrible."[4] But he embraced the job with enthusiasm. He hit the ground running and told CEO Sam Moore that he could turn Nelson Books around in three years.

It only took eighteen months.

In half the time he had promised, Nelson Books had not only improved under his leadership but was now at the top of the company's fourteen imprints. It was the fastest growing and most profitable, and it had the best team morale. It seemed like Michael couldn't stop succeeding.

Soon he brought home the biggest bonus check of his career up to that point. In fact, it was more than his annual salary. He couldn't wait to show it to his wife, as she was his biggest supporter and cheerleader. He knew she'd be thrilled.

Yet when he told her the good news, the look on her face didn't mirror his excitement. Instead, she said, "We need to talk."

Michael's heart sank.

With tears in her eyes, she said, "You know I love you, and I always appreciate everything you've done for our family. But I've got to tell you, you're never home. And even when you are, you're not really here. Your [five daughters] need you more than ever right now. Honestly, I feel like a single mom."

Michael reflected on that moment, and later said, "That was a huge gut kick to me, because here I was thinking that I'd reached the pinnacle of success. My dream job. I turned this division around. I made this huge amount of money. But it was a false summit."

He had achieved the traditional success he was after, but his family had suffered for it. For Michael, the attitude of "more, more, more" brought success in business but failure in his

THE FULFILLMENT
YOU'RE AFTER
never
COMES FROM
CHASING AFTER MORE.
IT *never*
COMES FROM
STRIVING.

TIM SCHURRER

personal life. It's easy enough to get a new job; it's harder to get a new family.

I hope we don't have to experience a moment like this to realize our definition of success has to change.

A CAREER IN SERVICE OF LIFE

A video titled "Twitter in Plain English" put Lee LeFever's business, Common Craft, on the map.[5] This was in 2008, right when social media was becoming popular, and Twitter was emerging as the top social platform. While more and more people joined Twitter, the majority of people had no idea what it was all about. Using an overhead camera and paper cutouts for the visuals, Lee's narration explained the basics of how Twitter functioned. It was so simple and easy to understand that people were sharing the video on YouTube, and it racked up millions of views. Soon after, Lee, along with his wife and business partner, Sachi, were getting calls from companies wanting them to explain their products and services in a simple way like they had for Twitter. Their second client was Google, and for them they created "Google Docs in Plain English," which gave them even more traction.[6]

Their business was off to a lightning-fast start, and within a couple of months they couldn't handle all the demand. It was at this point that they had to make a choice: Do they grow the business, or do they intentionally stay small? Lee ran the business with Sachi, and it was important that they protect their relationship first and foremost in whatever they decided.

Lee walked me through their decision-making process:

We have a lot of friends in Seattle who have worked in the startup world, and we've seen what it does to their lives. So many people that go into business are so focused on the money—are focused on the growth—that they lose sight of what it's doing to them at a personal level. And you sort of cross this point where if it's working, you're motivated to keep it going, and you're kind of trapped. And it might not be a terrible trap because you might be making a lot of money, but you find that there's no way out. Because of the business model, because of the expectations of the customers or having employees, you have a personal responsibility to keep the business going, even if you're done with it. Even if you want to change something fundamentally.[7]

Lee and Sachi made an intentional decision to stay small and agile, and did something a little crazy: they partnered with their competitors. Because there was so much demand for their business, they created the Common Craft Explainer Network. They charged a monthly fee for their competitors' information to be listed on their website, from which they would be funneled leads. Nine companies paid $750 a month to be listed. If you do the math, that's $81,000 in additional revenue each year, made possible by their decision to stay small. And even while channeling leads to other companies, they were able to hand-select their clients, such as LEGO, Ford, Intel, Dropbox, and Microsoft.

The thing to note here is they decided to run a business that serves the life they wanted to live rather than chase a version of success that didn't feel right to them. They intentionally passed on the green pastures. They forced themselves to lie down.

You see, lying down doesn't mean giving up. It's choosing to live in the way of the Secret Society by defining success for yourself, even if the rest of the world looks at you like you're crazy. Will you be misunderstood? Sure. Will you be mocked? Maybe. Will other people "beat" you? Yes. But only at a game you decided not to play. Those in the Secret Society know success has much more to do with creating a life you love than it does with getting to the top.

RECOVERING AFTER BEING KNOCKED DOWN

Sometimes you're pushed down. You don't realize you're caught in the Spotlight Mindset until it's too late. Like a bloated sheep, you need help, an intervention, if you want a chance at living a healthy life and career.

Remember my friend Andrew from chapter 2? Becoming a musician was a dream of his from when he was a teenager. But as he pursued it, his dream slowly led him down a path of depression, despair, and a near life crash. He was caught in the trap of the Spotlight Mindset, and fifteen years into his career, he was forced to give it up because of the anxiety and panic it caused him. On the outside it looked like things were going well—opportunities were all around him and his career was on a steady upswing—but he was experiencing sheep bloat. And it almost killed him.

For a season he walked away from music completely. He received some help from a counselor, he surrendered to the idea that he might never again step onstage to sing for people, and then he began to experience a breakthrough. The Spotlight Mindset he suffered from began to fade away. He recovered from his bouts with anxiety and panic. Then a miracle happened. He cautiously stepped back into music after a two-year hiatus. But this time he had a new perspective. He had learned to spot the traps of the Spotlight Mindset and avoided them at all costs. He had found a new path forward, a way to define success he'd never had before as a musician.

He wrote a song called "Jericho," which some radio people thought would do well. As an independent artist with a small team, they got the song in the hands of the right people, and more and more radio stations played it. The song was a success, and in February 2021, it hit number one on the charts. Andrew Ripp, an artist without a record label or a giant supporting team—who not too long before had been considering the idea of never playing music again—had the top song on the radio.

He posted on Instagram: "Jericho is officially a #1 song, folks. Watching the good Lord put these pieces together has been miraculous. Apparently when we let go of our dreams it makes room for even bigger ones."[8]

A CUSTOM DEFINITION OF SUCCESS

While this book has offered *the way of the Secret Society* as an idea for defining success, every person gets to choose what's right for them. There is no one-size-fits-all to this life. My hope is that you'll take what is helpful and feels right for the life you want to live, then riff off that until you're in a life and career that bring you joy and contentment.

Landing on your own definition of success is extremely important, but it can be difficult to hammer out a concrete list of things we want and value in our lives.

My list of values—the way I define success—came when I made a list called the "Secrets of Adulthood," which is an exercise I discovered in Gretchen Rubin's book *The Happiness Project*.[9]

My daughter was only a few months old when I read Gretchen's book, and while she slept in my arms, I typed my list of secrets into the Notes app on my phone, one by one. What started as a fun list quickly evolved into a more weighty list of things I hoped to teach my kids someday:

- Offer grace over guilt.
- Do things with excellence and the rest will take care of itself.
- Gratitude is better than resentment.
- Distance yourself from drama.
- Turn on jazz in the morning, the Archie Semple and Benny Goodman kind—a joyful mood will carry you throughout the day.*
- Go out of your way to encourage those behind the scenes.
- Be a firefighter—run toward the problem.
- Ask God to help you—don't try to do it alone.
- If you have a dream, chase it and don't let pessimists derail you.
- Stay out of debt.
- Try to make it to Augusta the first week of April every year for the Masters.
- Be where your feet are.
- Check your intentions whenever you're about to do or buy something.
- Be a lifelong learner—read books, listen to podcasts,

---

* If you want to hear my Jazz Mornings playlist, go to SecretSocietyBonus.com.

spend time with people who have been where you want to go, follow your curiosity.
- Focus on the process, not the result.
- Winning is fine but not at the expense of a relationship.
- Find a couple of friends you can be vulnerable with.
- Believe the best in others, even if you get screwed sometimes.
- Give yourself margin—feeling exhausted won't allow you to be at your best.

As I reread my list, the things I valued and the things I didn't became clearer to me, because what I value is an indication of the way I view success.

On my original list, I had come up with a hundred secrets that illuminated what was most important in my life. I found it interesting, for example, that not once did I write "make a lot of money." I don't have a problem with the idea of making a lot of money, but it's not a motivation for me the way it is for some people. Success, for me, doesn't have much to do with the number of zeros in my bank account.

But it wasn't just my view of money that was highlighted in this exercise. The list of secrets also showed me

- how much I value relationships, and how they need to be nurtured over time (decades, even);
- that I have an ability to be a conduit of joy and positivity for others;
- that excellent work isn't something to aspire to but the standard by which to do all things; and
- that hard times will come, but it's important to embrace challenges and respond with gratitude in every situation.

What's true of those in the Secret Society is that they have the courage to swim upstream, to define success for themselves rather than get caught in the trap of "more," which is sold to us by the Spotlight Mindset.

For Lee LeFever, success meant providing quality work for his clients by limiting his projects and referring the rest to his competitors. It meant a work-life balance. It meant he didn't hire more people and grow a large staff. For Andrew Ripp, it looked like taking a step away from his dream career to get some help, and in that time learn what a new definition of success could look like for him as a musician. For Michael Hyatt, it took a loving conversation with his wife to show him that success was not only about achievements during the workday.

Sometimes we believe our work lives are completely separate from the rest of our lives, that we can overwork ourselves, take on the world, and it won't affect our relationships or other interests outside of work. But as we've seen in this chapter and throughout this book, nothing could be further from the truth.

AS WE WALK THROUGH GREEN PASTURES

If you keep chasing after more, waiting to feel satisfied, to feel full, to feel like you've made it, you'll be eating until you make yourself sick. The fulfillment you're after will never come from striving. The elusive end that culture sells us will forever be just beyond our reach. I heard someone say that we are a country of people who are "always chasing 'yet.'" If so, it's up to us to choose how we want that journey to go.

The feeling of satisfaction and meaning in our lives and careers will come when we take the leap and define success for ourselves. When we have the courage to say, "This is the kind of life I want" and "I don't need *that* to be happy."

As we walk through green pastures with opportunities to get and have and chase and strive all around us, will we lie down (define success ourselves) or be pushed down (experience failure caused by the Spotlight Mindset)? One of these is a lot less painful than the other.

We have to define success for ourselves, and then live that way each and every day. It's the only thing that will keep us from sheep bloat.

The **ONLY ONES** AMONG YOU WHO WILL BE **REALLY HAPPY** ARE THOSE WHO HAVE *SOUGHT* and *FOUND* HOW TO SERVE.

ALBERT SCHWEITZER

12

AN **HONOR** TO **SERVE**

It's no surprise that while filming a television episode, lines and scenes get cut or moved around at the last minute. It's a constantly evolving project, and it's not uncommon for an actor to be given a set number of lines and appearances onscreen and for that to change at any time without notice.

If you look at it from the actor's perspective, you can see how that would be frustrating. But this process is necessary for the success of the show as a whole. The ultimate goal is for audiences to be engaged and entertained throughout, and the job of the showrunner is to do whatever it takes to create the best episodes possible.

Allan Heinberg is a writer and producer known for his work on *Grey's Anatomy, Sex and the City,* and *Gilmore Girls,* among others. He's often the person on set who makes the calls on how scenes should be moved around or when lines should be changed or cut.

There have been times when he makes these tough decisions and the actors are devastated. "But wait," they'd say, "yesterday I had all these lines. I don't have them now." They take it personally. Then, instead of accepting it, they spend time lobbying, trying to get their lines back in. Their security is threatened, and they react in a very normal, very human way.

What this causes, though, is a screeching halt to the creative production. Rather than Allan's energy going into additional editing or writing what needs to be written, he has to address how one actor is feeling about the new hand that's been dealt to them.

Allan told me, "What you really want them to say is, 'I'm just happy to be here. Use me in any way that you want.'"[1]

But we know by now that it is no small feat to resist the Spotlight Mindset. It is more challenging to serve than to be served. But I'd argue it's the key to a fulfilling life and career. And this . . . this is the path to the success we're really chasing after.

SUCCESS IS TO SERVE

What does it mean to serve? For many of us, the image of service conjures up scenes of hospitality. I immediately think of the waitstaff at a restaurant, people who serve you food. It is their job to serve people, to get customers what they want, to anticipate their needs. Perhaps you think of a valet, a concierge, or maybe the staff at a car wash.

But service is much broader than something that's done for money. I see it as an attitude, a mindset, an approach that motivates members of the Secret Society in everything they do. It's a way of seeing the world and a posture that asks, "How can I add value here?" or "How can I make your life easier, no matter who you are?" When you're in a mindset of service, you're not trying to figure out who is the most important person in the room (or hoping it's you). You're looking for ways to contribute. You're looking for needs to be met, and then considering if you can meet them.

Ten years ago, if you had asked me to describe a successful person, the word *service* would not have been part of my vocabulary. We talk about successful people as those with everything at their fingertips. They sit at the head of the table. They have assistants and staff to help them with whatever they want and need. I would have said that when you make it to the top, people wait on you and do what they can to make your life easier and more comfortable. So this should be the aspiration for all of us.

At least that's what I used to think.

But after learning the way of the Secret Society, I started to believe another story. I hope that after reading about the people in this book, you've come to the same conclusion: there's another way to define success.

What if we aren't here to get ahead? What if winning isn't the goal? What if success looks more like serving others and less like money, fame, or power? What if we viewed leadership positions as opportunities to serve more people, not less?

I want to leave you with a few more Secret Society members, people who have turned the popular understanding of success on its head. People who have found the meaning of success in service.

"BRING HIM HOME"

If you're a sports person, you may know Ernie Johnson, host of *Inside the NBA* with Charles Barkley, Kenny Smith, and Shaquille O'Neal. Ernie has won awards for his sports broadcasting and is a well-recognized sports journalist. There's no doubt he's made it to the top of his profession. He's in the spotlight, literally and metaphorically. But what's unique about Ernie is that his mentality is one of service, especially when you get some insight into his home life.

There was a time when Ernie's life couldn't have looked more successful. He had two healthy kids (a son and a daughter), a loving wife, and a great job. What could be missing?

Then, one evening in 1991, after Ernie got home from work, his wife, Cheryl, asked him, "You know what we need to do?"

Ernie responded, "Chicken or fish? I'm game for either tonight."

Cheryl said, "No, here's what I think we need to do. We need to go to Romania and adopt one of these kids out of an orphanage there. I watched *ABC News*, and these kids, they have it rough. They've been warehoused, especially these kids with any kind of abnormalities or birth defects."

The two of them seriously considered adoption, and not long after, Cheryl was on a plane to Romania, leaving their two children at home with Ernie. She was welcomed at the orphanage by a woman holding a three-year-old boy. She handed him to Cheryl, while saying in broken English, "Don't take. Boy is not good."

Later that night, she told Ernie about her day on the phone. "This kid is so much more than we can handle, but I don't know if I can go the rest of my life wondering what happened to that blond-haired kid in the orphanage," she said.

Ernie, on the other end of the line, simply said, "Bring him home."

They finalized the adoption and brought their new son, Michael, home to Atlanta. The first year was especially challenging, as Michael was treated for various ailments. Then a doctor told them, "Your son's got muscular dystrophy." If you know anything about muscular dystrophy, you know there's no cure, the muscles don't grow, they just waste away, and a lot of kids don't survive their teens. But Ernie and Cheryl didn't waste time wondering if this boy was worth helping. They saw he needed help and felt compelled to serve.

Ernie and Cheryl would serve Michael every day, helping him with everything from meals to getting dressed to taking him to the bathroom. This decision to adopt Michael changed their life, but in spite of all the inherent challenges of raising a child with muscular dystrophy, Ernie reflected, "Not for a second do you second-guess it or do you regret it. It's just like, okay, this is what we deal with? Here we go."[2]

The Johnsons have redefined what a successful life looks like. They were told Michael might not live past his teens, but because of their tremendous care and love for him, he lived a miraculous life of thirty-three years. Not only this, Ernie and Cheryl have adopted three more children. Modeling that success looks a whole lot like service, giving of themselves for the betterment of others.

Ernie doesn't model this approach only in how he serves his family. He himself was diagnosed with non-Hodgkin's lymphoma in 2003.[3] He fought the cancer and beat it, and now he wants to do whatever he can to help others who are on their own cancer journey. He said:

I think part of the responsibility that goes with [overcoming cancer] is that you help the next person through it. I can't tell you how many people who I've never met personally but have just talked to on the phone, because a friend of mine has said, "Hey, I got a buddy who's about to start chemo," and I say, "Well give me his number. We'll talk." And I'll tell him the same thing that was told to me when I was going through tests: you may have cancer but it doesn't have you.[4]

When Ernie was on our podcast at StoryBrand, we asked him, "If we want to have an extraordinary life, what is the thing that we need to remember every day?" His response tells you everything you need to know about how he lives his life: "Other people. That's what you have to remember. . . . I want to serve. I don't want to be this 'Hey, I'm a TV guy, what are you gonna do for me?' I want to be walking out the door, after having served Michael in the morning, and have my antenna up. So that I notice the people who need to have somebody to talk to or notice them."[5]

Ernie doesn't wait tables or work in hospitality. But he serves people every day of his life. He brings an attitude of "How can I be of help to others?" in all he does. Service is so essential to who Ernie is that it's difficult to separate that mindset from his success and happiness.

CREATING CULTURES OF SERVICE

What I've found is that the shared mindset of the Secret Society is contagious. As influential as it is to serve one's family and friends, it can be just as transformative for people in business to serve their coworkers and customers. When entire teams and organizations adopt this new mindset, world-class cultures begin to emerge. As you start practicing the way of the Secret Society, you'll have opportunities to not only change your own mindset but to help others adopt this mindset as well.

Alan Mulally, former CEO of Ford, turned the company around by focusing on service. When Ford brought him on in

2006, "the company was preparing to post the biggest annual loss in its 103-year history—$12.7 billion."[6] Then, under Mulally, the company posted a profit in 2009 and for several consecutive years after that. Talk about a transformation!

The secret to the huge turnaround? Getting every employee onboard, seeing themselves as a team, and fostering a culture of cooperation and service. And this attitude starts at the top. Alan summarized his leadership perspective:

> At the most fundamental level, it is an honor to serve—at whatever type or size of organization you are privileged to lead, whether it is a for-profit or nonprofit. It is an honor to serve. Starting from that foundation, it is important to have a compelling vision and a comprehensive plan. Positive leadership—conveying the idea that there is always a way forward—is so important, because that is what you are here for—to figure out how to move the organization forward. Critical to doing that is reinforcing the idea that everyone is included. Everyone is part of the team and everyone's contribution is respected, so everyone should participate. When people feel accountable and included, it is more fun. It is just more rewarding to do things in a supportive environment.[7]

Employees should not feel alone or pressured to solve problems on their own. Alan sees leadership as a responsibility to empower people, to help them with their responsibilities, and, in effect, to help the entire team function. Instead of coming in with a "my way or the highway" attitude, his belief in service transformed the organization and turned a profit.

The Home Depot's executive leadership mirrors much of what Alan modeled at Ford. They use a diagram called the inverted pyramid as a reminder of the company's philosophy from its founding: "Put customers and associates first, and the rest will take care of itself."[8] At the bottom (the point of the inverted pyramid) is the CEO, beneath corporate support, beneath field support, beneath front-line associates, beneath customers. Each level supports and serves the next. But instead of leadership at the top being the ones who are served, they've flipped the triangle on its head, with customers at the top. The mentality of this company is what has propelled them to success.

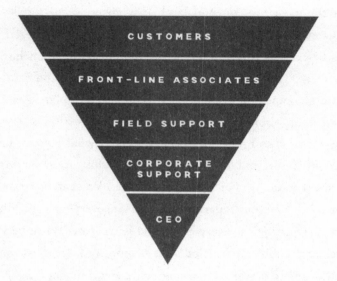

The greatest leaders see themselves at the bottom, supporting everyone else, not at the top. Those with healthy company cultures are ready to serve others. This is the way of the Secret Society.

Think of what we could accomplish if we could change the cultures in our offices and on our teams. Think of how that mindset shift would impact every person who works with you and who interacts with your brand. You might find yourself excited to go to work and motivated to help others succeed.

SERVICE IN HOLLYWOOD?

You might wonder how Allan Heinberg got to the position he's in as a writer and producer of television shows. From the time he was a kid, he was an actor, and like many actors, he had aspirations to make it to Broadway. His dream came true when, at twenty-four years old, he was given a part in the Broadway production of *Laughter on the 23rd Floor*, written by Neil Simon.

His experience, though, wasn't what he had prepared for. "You think that once you get to Broadway and are in a Broadway show, you've made it. But I saw how unhappy a lot of the people were—even the stars of the show—and thought, I don't think this is going to make me happy long-term," he told me.[9]

Allan had started writing plays in college, but he wanted to continue to sing and act. Even when he got to New York and was in a Broadway show, he was living this budding playwright life. In fact, one of the plays he'd written was chosen to be produced off Broadway. This meant he was doing rehearsals and rewrites for the play by day, and then performing as an actor on Broadway by night. This gave him the experience to directly compare what it was like as an actor and as a creator writing the stories others would ultimately perform.

"The joy I had from acting, even on Broadway, was limited," he said. So he decided to follow his passion as a writer. Soon he became a sought-after screenwriter. He found success, and with it every opportunity to "make it about himself," as was often the temptation as a Broadway actor.

Allan said, "A ton of writers make it about them. They tell the actors, crew, press . . . 'Nobody knows how to do this but me.'" But he approaches projects with a very different perspective.

When he's recruited to work on a project, he asks, "How can I best serve you and your interests and your slate?"

After telling me this, Allan smiled, and said, "When you say the word 'serve' in the Hollywood culture, people look at you a little funny."[10]

But it's this genuine posture of service that has differentiated him from others in the industry. That, paired with his remarkable writing talent, has given him unparalleled opportunities. He was asked to write the screenplay for the feature film *Wonder Woman*, which was an honor of a lifetime because of how much he enjoyed the DC Comics character. (Fun fact: When I first met Allan in 2009, his business card had a picture of Wonder Woman on the back. This was *years* before he was asked to write that screenplay.)

Allan is so focused on serving each project he's a part of that people jump at the opportunity to work with him. He's not consumed with his ego. He's not someone who demands attention. He focuses on making quality work. And because of that, he attracts attention left and right, which he's postured to receive with humility and gratitude.

As you continue to live in the way of the Secret Society, ask yourself, "Is there a way I can serve here?"

LEARNING TO CLIMB FASTER

When you make the radical shift to this new mindset, the way of the Secret Society, success is already yours.

– Instead of chasing opportunities on your pursuit for "more," you will be looking for opportunities where you can best serve.

WHAT IF

SUCCESS LOOKS

· MORE LIKE ·

SERVING OTHERS

& LESS LIKE

MONEY, FAME,

OR POWER?

TIM SCHURRER

- Instead of feeling restless about your job or the role you play on the team, you'll wake up excited about your work and confident in your contributions.
- You'll be all about the assist.
- By asking "Who am I here for?" and then solving problems for others, you'll make a meaningful impact in the world.
- By getting lost in the work and giving away the credit, you'll find fulfillment in a job well done.
- You'll live into your own definition of success and enjoy your work (and life) again.

Albert Schweitzer said, "I don't know what your destiny will be. Some of you will perhaps occupy remarkable positions. Perhaps some of you will become famous by your pens, or as artists. But I know one thing: the only ones among you who will be really happy are those who have sought and found how to serve."[11] I don't know about you, but I'd rather be happy and successful on my own terms than miserable and successful by everyone else's. The Secret Society has this figured out. This is the kind of success that matters most.

Each chapter in this book has given you a tool to use in the fight against the Spotlight Mindset, the unhealthy desire for attention and recognition. But there's one more thing you need to know, and it may be the most important of them all: we can't do this alone.

In the years I spent writing this book, I was up against some of the most challenging situations of my life. In those moments I felt miserable, and there were times I felt helpless. But as the years passed and these tools were uncovered, I began to apply them whenever I was in a metaphorical hole. These tools were the ladders I used to get back to a healthy mindset.

The lesson here is to take inventory of the content in this book and become familiar with the tools you now have at your disposal—your ladders, if you will. But if I'm honest, these ladders alone are only so effective. You can apply all the mental tricks and still find yourself in holes from time to time. That, then, becomes the question: How can you learn to climb out faster?

The answer is not a thing but a person. It could be a friend or a mentor or the Secret Society or God. It's been a combination of all of these for me as I've learned we can't do this alone.

A good friend of mine told me, "When I am at my best, I refuse to fly solo. At my worst, I isolate and muscle through life on my own. It is a humble and wise posture when I admit I need help and support."

We need others to help us when we fall. When we fall, *they* are the ones handing us the ladder.

At the start, the ladders seemed long, and it would often take me a while to get out of holes. But equipped with the tools to guide me out and friends to support me along the way, I'm learning to climb faster. These days I am able to get out of some holes within minutes, which before might have taken days or weeks.

When you feel an unhealthy desire for attention and recognition or that itch of restlessness and discontent, I hope you know there's a way out of the hole. I hope you take hold of these tools and use them, until it becomes easy and natural to you. I hope you experience the contentment and fulfillment of a life of service, and that it motivates you to fight against the Spotlight Mindset, no matter how challenging that can be at times.

May we be the people who learn to climb quickly. And may we also be the people who hand ladders to others, encouraging them as they climb to the top.

WHEN I FIND MYSELF IN THE GRASP OF THE SPOTLIGHT MINDSET — A METAPHORICAL HOLE — THE TOOLS & MINDSET SHIFTS I'VE LEARNED FROM THE SECRET SOCIETY ARE THE LADDERS I USE TO CLIMB OUT.

TIM SCHURRER

LIVING IN THE WAY
OF THE SECRET SOCIETY

I would love to tell you that you can overcome the Spotlight Mindset by following a simple three-step process. And I wish I could promise you that after following those three steps, you'd never struggle with it again.

But as you've already learned, the Spotlight Mindset is not a problem to solve; it's a tension to manage. You won't wake up one day and say, "Well, I did it. I don't struggle with an unhealthy desire for attention and recognition anymore. Oh, and the symptoms of a Spotlight Mindset? Striving, comparing, damaged relationships, fear of failure, seeking validation, selfishness, seeking influence? Those don't show up in my life now. I'm all set."

I hate to break it to you, but that won't happen. The truth is, we'll oscillate between the Spotlight Mindset and the way of the Secret Society regularly. Overcoming the Spotlight Mindset is not something we do once; it's something we get better and better at over time.

When I find myself in the grasp of the Spotlight Mindset—a metaphorical hole—the tools and mindset shifts I've learned from the Secret Society are the ladders I use to climb out. Changing my mindset is a practice, and something I try to keep top of mind so I can "stay in shape" and quickly climb out of the holes I find myself in.

My friend Koula Callahan is a yoga instructor. I asked her what happens if her regular students just stop. What happens if they are out of practice?

First, they lose the physical component, she told me: strength, endurance, mobility, and flexibility. Second, they lose the mental component. This is when my ears perked up.

> They become irritable and agitated whenever they experience anything challenging, whether that's a yoga pose or something hard at work or in their personal lives. However, the more they engage in their yoga practice, the more they're able to willingly enter into something that's challenging and not let it throw them out of whack. By welcoming the discomfort and challenge of yoga, welcoming and engaging challenges in other areas of their lives becomes an immediate, subconscious response.[1]

That's what we're aiming for with the way of the Secret Society, to get to a place where living this way is an immediate, subconscious response.

The opportunities to engage in this practice are available to all of us. As such, it's imperative that we become familiar with the tools at our disposal to help us along the way. On the next two pages, you'll find a list of paradigm shifts that will make it easy for you to reference *the way of the Secret Society.* Refer to it whenever you want a quick reminder.

By keeping current with all you've come to know by reading this book, you'll be equipped to have more healthy thoughts, be quicker to serve others, and make a habit of defining success for yourself. Not only this, your immediate subconscious response when faced with challenges will be that of the Secret Society.

You can keep coming back to these tools. You don't have to buy them. You don't have to go anywhere to get them. They're yours. You have everything you need to enjoy your work (and life) again.

PARADIGM SHIFTS

	The Spotlight Mindset	The Way of the Secret Society
CHAPTER 1 The Secret Society	We have to be the one people are talking about to be successful.	We execute our role with excellence, even if that means fading into the background.
CHAPTER 2 The Spotlight Mindset	We believe that chasing after money, fame, and power is the only way to have a successful life and career.	We see an alternative path to success, one that's not highlighted by our culture. We know an unhealthy desire for attention and recognition will make us restless, jealous, discontent, and unhappy.
CHAPTER 3 Success Is in the Assist	We focus on individual success even at the expense of others.	We prioritize assisting others, setting them up to win.
CHAPTER 4 Playing by the Wrong Scoreboard	We need to rank high on the list of culture's scoreboards. Our position on the social hierarchy motivates our thoughts and actions.	Culture's scoreboards don't get our energy or attention. We're willing to swim upstream in that regard while recognizing that life is not a zero-sum game. We are committed to collaboration over competition, and we believe we don't need to beat anyone to win.
CHAPTER 5 Looking for a Little Bit of Recognition	Our value is contingent on recognition, and so we will do whatever we can to get onstage, be seen, and be recognized.	We regularly give recognition to others, regardless of whether we ever receive it in return. We do not link our worth to getting noticed.
CHAPTER 6 You Don't Need a Stage	We need to have some kind of stage or platform.	We measure ourselves not by where we're standing but by the people we're impacting. One life at a time.

PARADIGM SHIFTS

	The Spotlight Mindset	The Way of the Secret Society
CHAPTER 7 **Let a Problem Be Your Solution**	We look for people to solve our problems, constantly thinking, *What's in it for me?*	We look for ways to solve other people's problems, asking, "What problem can I solve for someone else?"
CHAPTER 8 **Get Lost in the Work**	We are fixated on a particular vision of success—namely, the end result.	We have learned to focus on the process, surrender the outcome, and let the results take care of themselves.
CHAPTER 9 **Embrace Challenges and Learn from Failure**	We believe success is a steady incline to the top. Problems are to be avoided or ignored.	We believe success is not a straight line up or a guarantee, but instead it is found in embracing challenges and learning from failure.
CHAPTER 10 **When You Don't Mind Who Gets the Credit**	We need the credit for our work.	We don't mind who gets the credit.
CHAPTER 11 **When Is Enough, Enough?**	We never seem to have enough, and as such we never stop chasing and striving. We are at risk of sheep bloat.	We have learned to define success for ourselves and have found contentment in that. We are willing to lie down in green pastures for the sake of our health and relationships.
CHAPTER 12 **An Honor to Serve**	Our modus operandi is to serve ourselves and believe that is the way to get ahead and get everything we want out of life.	We serve others, and as a result we have found meaning, joy, and fulfillment in our lives and careers.

To download these paradigm shifts as a PDF along with other
bonus resources, go to **SecretSocietyBonus.com**

AS THE LEADER
OF A TEAM

If you are in a position of leadership, you know there's nothing more important than your team. A company should be a group of people coming together with their best effort for the betterment of whatever goal or project they're working on. The problem is that our default as humans is to think only about ourselves and to operate from a Spotlight Mindset. How, then, can we lead our teams to operate in the way of the Secret Society and adopt this practice on a more regular basis? How can a team view of success become the norm and serving others become the focus?

By providing a copy of *The Secret Society of Success* for every member on your team and walking them through each chapter of this book, you'll start to notice a shift in their hearts and minds around these concepts. While it won't be an overnight transformation, there's nothing more important than starting the journey and inviting your team to live in the way of the Secret Society.

I'm grateful for your desire to serve others. If I can ever be of help, or if you'd like for me to speak to your organization, don't hesitate to send me an email at timschurrer@gmail.com.

SHOUT-OUTS

While my name happens to be the one on the cover, what should really be there alongside it is the long list of names I'm about to share with you. It takes a team of people for projects like this to come to life, and this book wouldn't have been possible without each and every one of these friends.

Donald Miller—I've heard it said that "you cannot be what you cannot see." So the idea of writing a book and speaking to groups of people wouldn't have crossed my mind as a career path to pursue had I not seen you model it so brilliantly first. Getting to work as your right-hand man for almost a decade was the opportunity of a lifetime and has forever shaped the trajectory of my life. And with this book, you've been my biggest advocate. I'm grateful.

Bob Goff—It was at one of your workshops that I said my big dream out loud for the first time: "I want to write a book." And after that, you called, emailed, and texted me dozens of times asking for the latest on my writing project. It was the encouragement I needed to keep going.

Ben Ortlip—As soon as you heard I was writing a book, you drove from Atlanta to spend a day with me to map out the content. The counsel you gave me in the early stages of this book shaped it in a massive way.

Bryan Norman—The journey from idea to book contract to publication date only has about a thousand steps. I needed a guide and a champion, and you've been both.

Ally Fallon and Annie Kyle—Getting to write this book with you was an unbelievable experience. I have tears in my eyes thinking about the work we did together. You've modeled the way of the Secret Society with every word you helped put on the page. Thank you, friends.

Kyle Reid—You've been in my corner from day one. No matter what I needed help with, you've said yes before I even finished asking.

Doug Keim—So much of this book was shaped by our conversations. It wasn't an accident that our paths crossed when they did. I'm grateful for you and the impact you've had in my life.

Matt Lehman—I've been the (self-proclaimed) president of your fan club for several years now. Getting the opportunity to work with you on the book cover design was a dream come true.

Margot Groner—The quotes you designed and the font you created for this book were an incredible addition. You're insanely talented. I am so happy you said yes to this project.

Steve Moakler and Al Andrews—I don't think you realize how much I've learned from each of you about living in the way of the Secret Society. You showed me how to define success long before I attempted to put it into words.

Brigitta Nortker and Sujin Hong—You have shown me the power of working with a great team of editors. You are true professionals and have made this book so, so much better. Can't thank you enough.

Karen Jackson, Claire Drake, Sara Broun, Sarah Van Cleve, and Jennifer Smith—It's one thing to write a book and another to get it out into the world. I appreciate all the energy you've invested to get this book into as many hands as possible.

Tim Paulson, Emily Ghattas, Phoebe Wetherbee, Kristina Juodenas, Aryana Hendrawan, Sydney Mathieu, Jamekra Willis, Chernal Patton, and the rest of the team at Nelson Books—I've been energized by your excitement around this project from the very beginning. Thank you, thank you, thank you.

Ed Curtis, Lisa Grimenstein, Vanessa Christensen, Elisa Stanford, and Sara Benner—You've done so much work behind the scenes to make this book easy to read. I've seen the before and after and am grateful for how you've executed your part of the project with excellence.

Dae Eriksson, Candice Watkins, and Ben Malcolmson—Becoming friends with you was the beginning of me discovering the Secret Society. You're some of the most humble and talented people I know who have made a career out of serving others.

Koula Callahan, J.J. Peterson, Kyle Willis, Tyler Ginn, Carey Murdock, Emily Pastina, and the rest of the StoryBrand team—Thank you for what you each contributed to this book in big and small ways. The way of the Secret Society was the culture we created together every day at work. I wouldn't have been able to write this book without first having had the opportunity to put it into practice while working alongside each of you.

Alex Collins—While you're no longer with us, I'll never forget all of the times we spent talking through the ideas in this book. You were always eager to hear about whatever chapter I was working on and were an incredible sounding board. I miss you, Pal.

Richard Goff—You wrote me a check to pre-order my book more than two years before it even came out. You've shown me what it looks like to be a champion for your friends and their dreams.

All the people I used as examples in this book—Thank you for inspiring me and letting me share your stories. I've learned about what it means to be in the Secret Society from watching you.

Mom—You've helped me believe that anything is possible. I never would have chased my dreams had it not been for your optimism and unrelenting support. You've shown me the kind of parent I want to be to my kids as they get older and pursue what's important to them.

Katie—I have the privilege of watching you live in the way of the Secret Society each and every day with our family and friends. Serving others is what you're all about, and you do it with joy. It's inspiring. Also, you've been my ride or die throughout this book writing process. I love my life because I get to live it with you.

And finally, to you—I wrote this book to start a conversation about redefining success. It means the world to me that you bought the book and invested the time to read the entire thing. It's now up to you to keep the conversation going with your friends and colleagues. I can't wait to hear the stories of how your life has been impacted as you learn to live in the way of the Secret Society.

NOTES

Introduction: The Success You're Looking For

1. "Achieving Fame, Wealth, and Beauty Are Psychological Dead Ends, Study Says," University of Rochester, May 14, 2009, http://www.rochester.edu/news/show.php?id=3377.

2. Louise Story, "Anywhere the Eye Can See, It's Likely to See an Ad," *New York Times*, January 15, 2007, https://www.nytimes.com/2007/01/15/business/media/15everywhere.html.

3. Donald Miller, *Building a StoryBrand: Clarify Your Message So Customers Will Listen* (New York: HarperCollins Leadership, 2017), 9.

4. Brad Montague, conversation with author, July 31, 2019.

Chapter 1: The Secret Society

1. J. R. Moehringer, *Sutton* (New York: Hyperion, 2012), 33.

2. Marina Koren, "Michael Collins Liked His Alone Time," *Atlantic*, July 18, 2019, https://www.theatlantic.com/science/archive/2019/07/michael-collins-moon-landing-apollo-11/594238/.

3. Rick Dandes, "Collins 'Perfectly Happy' with His Role in Apollo 11 Mission," *Salem News*, July 20, 2019, https://www.salemnews .com/news/collins-perfectly-happy-with-his-role-in-apollo-11 -mission/article_3d4ef2a1-33fe-5a86-8f09-f08219ad9814.html.

4. James Higa described his job at Apple Inc. as "special ops" on his LinkedIn profile. Accessed October 22, 2021, https://www .linkedin.com/in/jameshiga/.

5. "Biography," Viola Spolin (official website), accessed October 22, 2021, https://www.violaspolin.org/bio.

Chapter 2: The Spotlight Mindset

1. Tim Arnold, *The Power of Healthy Tension: Overcome Chronic Issues and Conflicting Values* (Amherst, MA: HRD Press, 2017), 13.

Chapter 3: Success Is in the Assist

1. Bob Goff, *Love Does: Discover a Secretly Incredible Life in an Ordinary World* (Nashville: Thomas Nelson, 2012).

2. Dan Heath, *Upstream: The Quest to Solve Problems Before They Happen* (New York: Bantam, 2020).

3. Daniel H. Pink, *Drive: The Surprising Truth About What Motivates Us* (New York: Riverhead Books, 2009).

4. "About," LeBron James Family Foundation, accessed October 29, 2021, https://www.lebronjamesfamilyfoundation .org/about/.

5. Erica L. Green, "LeBron James Opened a School That Was Considered an Experiment: It's Showing Promise," *New York Times*, April 12, 2019, https://www.nytimes.com/2019/04/12 /education/lebron-james-school-ohio.html.

Chapter 4: Playing by the Wrong Scoreboard

1. Jordan B. Peterson, *12 Rules for Life: An Antidote to Chaos* (Toronto: Random House Canada, 2018), 45.

2. Peterson, *12 Rules for Life*, 53.

3. "Social Status Is Hard-Wired into the Brain, Study Shows," PBS News Hour, April 25, 2008, https://www.pbs.org/newshour /science/science-jan-june08-status_04-25.

4. Caroline F. Zink et al., "Know Your Place: Neural Processing of Social Hierarchy in Humans," *Neuron* 58, no. 2 (April 24, 2008): 273–83, https://www.ncbi.nlm.nih.gov/pmc/articles/PMC2430590/.

5. Zink et al., "Know Your Place."

6. Liz Mineo, "Good Genes Are Nice, but Joy Is Better," *Harvard Gazette*, April 11, 2017, https://news.harvard.edu/gazette/story /2017/04/over-nearly-80-years-harvard-study-has-been-showing -how-to-live-a-healthy-and-happy-life/.

7. Mineo, "Good Genes Are Nice."

8. "Social Status Is Hard-Wired into the Brain."

9. Robert Waldinger, "What Makes a Good Life? Life Lessons from the Longest Study on Happiness," TEDxBeaconStreet, November 2015, video, 5:49, https://www.ted.com/talks /robert_waldinger_what_makes_a_good_life_lessons_from _the_longest_study_on_happiness/transcript.

10. Adam Grant, *Give and Take: A Revolutionary Approach to Success* (New York: Viking, 2013), 4.

11. Grant, *Give and Take*, 15–16.

Chapter 5: Looking for a Little Bit of Recognition

1. Oprah Winfrey, *The Wisdom of Sundays: Life-Changing Insights from Super Soul Conversations* (New York: Flatiron Books, 2017), Kindle loc. 176.

2. "Dan Heath—How to Create Powerful Moments for the People You Serve," January 15, 2018, in *Business Made Simple with Donald Miller*, podcast, https://podcasts.apple.com/us/podcast /79-dan-heath-how-to-create-powerful-moments-for-people /id1092751338?i=1000399879627&mt=2.

3. Indra Nooyi, "PepsiCo CEO: I Write Letters to Parents of My Executives," Bloomberg Quicktake, December 7, 2016, YouTube video, https://www.youtube.com/watch?v=hKaoQpG29RQ.

4. Chris Hedges, *Empire of Illusion: The End of Literacy and the Triumph of Spectacle* (New York: Nation Books, 2009), 22.

Chapter 6: You Don't Need a Stage

1. Jon Acuff, *Soundtracks: The Surprising Solution to Overthinking* (Grand Rapids, MI: Baker Books, 2021).

2. Guy Raz, "How I Built This," NPR, February 11, 2019, https://www.npr.org/2019/02/08/692781997/toms-blake-mycoskie.

3. Raz, "How I Built This."

4. "A Single Candle Cuts Through the Darkest Night," Thistle Farms, accessed October 29, 2021, https://thistlefarms.org/pages/our-mission.

5. Regina, "How Love Heals," Thistle Farms, video, 1:05, accessed October 29, 2021, https://thistlefarms.org/pages/our-mission.

6. Becca Stevens, "How Love Heals," Thistle Farms, video, 1:25, accessed October 29, 2021, https://thistlefarms.org/pages/our -mission.

7. Jennifer Clinger, *Delivered: The Fragmented Memories of a Former Streetwalker* (Scotts Valley, CA: CreateSpace, 2018), 16.

8. Clinger, *Delivered*, 15.

9. Becca Stevens, *Love Heals* (Nashville: Thomas Nelson, 2017), 2.

10. "Tattoos, Balding, and Window Seats—Drew Holcomb," September 2020, in *Dadville with Dave Barnes and Jon McLaughlin*, podcast, https://podcasts.apple.com/us /podcast/tattoos-balding-and-window-seats-drew-holcomb /id1517698133?i=1000492919870.

11. Drew Holcomb, "Legacy of Jay" (senior thesis, University of Tennessee, Knoxville, 2003), 158, https://trace.tennessee.edu/cgi /viewcontent.cgi?article=1025&context=utk_interstp3.

Chapter 7: Let a Problem Be Your Solution

1. "About Fred Rogers," Mister Rogers' Neighborhood (website), accessed November 5, 2021, https://www.misterrogers.org /about-fred-rogers/.

2. Lin-Manuel Miranda, "My Shot," *Hamilton: An American Musical*, 2015.

3. "Some Words from Artists," Porter's Call, accessed November 5, 2021, https://www.porterscall.com/words-from-artists.

Chapter 8: Get Lost in the Work

1. Michael Brody-Waite, "Great Leaders Do What Drug Addicts Do," TEDxNashville, March 2018, video, https://www.ted.com/talks

/michael_brody_waite_great_leaders_do_what_drug_addicts
_do?language=en.

2. Brody-Waite, "Great Leaders Do What Drug Addicts Do."

3. Chris McChesney, Sean Covey, and Jim Huling, *The 4 Disciplines of Execution: Achieving Your Wildly Important Goals* (New York: Free Press, 2012), 62–63.

4. "Inside a NASCAR Pit Crew at the Daytona 500," theCHIVE, March 21, 2017, YouTube video, https://www.youtube.com /watch?v=U1uXtNQEdwU.

5. "Changing the Game of Baseball," Savannah Bananas (website), accessed November 5,2021, https://thesavannahbananas.com /banana-ball-rules/.

6. Annie F. Downs, *That Sounds Fun: The Joys of Being an Amateur, the Power of Falling in Love, and Why You Need a Hobby* (Grand Rapids, MI: Revell, 2021), 43.

7. Merriam-Webster Online, s.v. "amateur," accessed November 5, 2021, https://www.merriam-webster.com/dictionary/amateur.

8. Jim Clifton, "The World's Broken Workplace," *Chairman's Blog*, Gallup, June 13, 2017, https://news.gallup.com/opinion/chairman /212045/world-broken-workplace.aspx.

9. Donald Miller, *Scary Close: Dropping the Act and Finding True Intimacy* (Nashville: Nelson Books, 2014).

Chapter 9: Embrace Challenges and Learn from Failure

1. Donald Miller, *A Million Miles in a Thousand Years: What I Learned While Editing My Life* (Nashville: Thomas Nelson, 2009), 48.

2. Scott Hamilton, "Make It Count: Scott Hamilton Discusses His Cancer Journey," Cure Today, June 6, 2020, https://www .curetoday.com/view/make-it-count-scott-hamilton-discusses -his-cancer-journey.

3. Scott Hamilton, "Scott Hamilton: Training for Olympic Gold," *Encyclopedia Britannica*, August 23, 2002, https://www .britannica.com/topic/Olympic-training-760104.

4. Scott Hamilton, *Finish First: Winning Changes Everything* (Nashville: W Publishing, 2018), Kindle loc. 1049.

5. Lanny Bassham, *With Winning in Mind*, 3rd ed. (Flower Mound, TX: Mental Management Systems, 2011).

6. Ben Crane, conversation with author, August 8, 2016.

7. Hamilton, *Finish First*, Kindle loc. 1076.

8. Blake Mycoskie, "Lesson No. 2: Find Opportunity in Challenges," *Next Steps* (newsletter), accessed November 5, 2021, https://nextsteps.blakemycoskie.com/lesson/no-2-find -opportunity-in-challenges.

9. Hamilton, *Finish First*, Kindle loc. 1299.

Chapter 10: When You Don't Mind Who Gets the Credit

1. "Alyssa Mastromonaco," Council for Advancement and Support of Education, accessed November 8, 2021, https://www.case.org /node/8022.

2. "Alyssa Mastromonaco, Former White House Deputy Chief of Staff," Into the Gloss, accessed November 8, 2021, https:// intothegloss.com/2019/03/alyssa-mastromonaco-interview/.

3. Alyssa Mastromonaco, *Who Thought This Was a Good Idea?: And Other Questions You Should Have Answers to When You Work in the White House* (New York: Twelve, 2017), 130.

4. Mastromonaco, *Who Thought This Was a Good Idea?*, 176.

5. Tim Cook, "Apple Watch: Will It Revolutionize the Personal Device?," interview by David Muir, *Nightline*, ABC, September 10, 2014, YouTube video, https://youtube.com /watch?v=4QUpQC4zrhU.

6. Ronald Reagan, "Remarks at a Meeting of the White House Conference for a Drug Free America," February 29, 1988, Reagan Quotes and Speeches, Ronald Reagan Presidential Foundation, https://www.reaganfoundation.org/ronald-reagan /reagan-quotes-speeches/remarks-at-a-meeting-of-the-white -house-conference-for-a-drug-free-america/.

7. John Donne, "Devotions upon Emergent Occasions," Meditation 17 (1624), in *The Works of John Donne*, ed. Henry Alford, vol. 3 (London: Parker, 1839), http://www.luminarium.org/sevenlit /donne/meditation17.php.

8. Sarah (@sarahbible), Instagram, May 9, 2021, https://www .instagram.com/p/COrQLcwhPt0/.

9. Gertrude Stein, *Everybody's Autobiography* (New York: Random House, 1937), 289.

Chapter 11: When Is Enough, Enough?

1. Jason Strand, "I'm Tired," sermon, March 14, 2021, in *Eagle Brook Church Podcast*, https://eaglebrookchurch.com/media /past-messages/im-tired/.
2. Laurie Ball-Gisch, "Prevent Sheep Bloat by Managing Your Flock: Bloat in Sheep Can Be Deadly," *Countryside*, September 27, 2021, https://www.iamcountryside.com/sheep /prevent-sheep-bloat/.
3. Psalm 23:1–2 NIV.
4. "Michael Hyatt—Can You Grow Your Business Working Six Hour Days?" March 29, 2021, in *Business Made Simple with Donald Miller*, podcast, https://podcasts.apple.com/us/podcast /michael-hyatt-can-you-grow-your-business-working-six /id1092751338?i=1000514837610.
5. "Twitter in Plain English," Common Craft, March 5, 2008, YouTube video, https://www.youtube.com/watch?v =ddO9idmax0o.
6. "Google Docs in Plain English," Common Craft, October 19, 2007, YouTube video, https://www.youtube.com/watch?v =muVUA-sKcc4.
7. Lee LeFever, conversation with author, May 20, 2021.
8. Andrew Ripp (@andrewripp), "Jericho is officially a #1 song, folks," Instagram photo, February 23, 2021, https://www .instagram.com/p/CLo-FL1Bqv7.
9. Gretchen Rubin, *The Happiness Project: Or, Why I Spent a Year Trying to Sing in the Morning, Clean My Closets, Fight Right, Read Aristotle, and Generally Have More Fun* (New York: Harper, 2009).

Chapter 12: An Honor to Serve

1. Allan Heinberg, conversation with author, March 6, 2021.
2. "Ernie Johnson—3 Life Lessons That Will Inspire You to Slow Down and Live Differently," May 2017, in *Business Made Simple with Donald Miller*, podcast, http://buildingastorybrand.com /episode-44/.

3. "Ernie Johnson Shares His Cancer Story," Athletes in Action USA, March 13, 2007, YouTube video, https://youtube.com /watch?v=ud-b8iCm2oE.

4. "Ernie Johnson—3 Life Lessons That Will Inspire You."

5. "Ernie Johnson—3 Life Lessons That Will Inspire You."

6. Alan Mulally and Rik Kirkland, "Leading in the 21st Century: An Interview with Ford's Alan Mulally," McKinsey & Company, November 1, 2013, https://www.mckinsey.com/business-functions /strategy-and-corporate-finance/our-insights/leading-in-the-21st -century-an-interview-with-fords-alan-mulally#.

7. Mulally and Kirkland, "Leading in the 21st Century."

8. "Built from All the Right Materials," Home Depot, accessed November 8, 2021, https://corporate.homedepot.com/about.

9. Allan Heinberg, conversation with author, March 6, 2021.

10. Allan Heinberg, conversation with author, May 23, 2019.

11. Steve Perisho, "Schweitzer on Service," *Liber Locorum Communium* (blog), October 25, 2010, http://liberlocorumcommunium.blogspot .com/2010/10/schweitzer-on-service.html; quoted from Albert Schweitzer, "The Meaning of Ideals in Life," speech, Silcoates School, Wakefield, England, December 3, 1935.

Appendix: Living in the Way of the Secret Society

1. Koula Callahan, conversation with the author, May 20, 2021.

ABOUT THE AUTHOR

Tim Schurrer knows what it takes to build a winning team. He spent almost a decade of his career launching two brands—StoryBrand and Business Made Simple—as COO alongside *New York Times* bestselling author Donald Miller.

In that time, Tim and the team accomplished the following:

- Grew the business from $250K to $16.5M in annual revenue.
- Generated more than 20 million podcast downloads.
- Launched multiple bestselling books and on-demand video courses.
- Produced dozens of events, from a 2,400-person conference to a 5,500-person livestream.
- And, most importantly, built a culture where people loved

their work and would do whatever it took to help one another and their customers win.

Before his time at StoryBrand and Business Made Simple, Tim worked at TOMS as well as Apple Inc. He is the host of the *Build a Winning Team* podcast, where he offers listeners actionable advice as he interviews some of the top leaders in business.

Tim lives in Nashville, Tennessee, with his wife, Katie, and their two kids.

CONNECT WITH TIM

If you've resonated with this book, Tim would love to hear from you. Send him an email (timschurrer@gmail.com) or leave him a comment on Instagram (@timschurrer). You can also find more information about booking him to speak at your event or to your team on his website: BuildAWinningTeam.com.

Get **actionable advice** from some of the **top leaders in business**

Subscribe today wherever you listen to podcasts